ISBN: 978-1-7394874-0-9

Coding: the 21st century's most valuable skill

Simon Monk

To my mother Anne Kemp
1924-2022.

Foreword

Almost every aspect of modern life relies on software code. Many children are learning to code at school, as this is being recognised as an important skill that many people will use in their work and private lives.

Whereas there are many books that will teach you a particular programming language, this book sets this core skill in the context of both the software tools people use and the software industry as a whole.

The book does not assume any prior knowledge of coding. Part I of the book aims to teach a basic knowledge of Python as well as other technologies that are typical of real-life development such as databases and web frameworks.

Part II of the book will let you in on all the things that happen in software development teams and what a coder actually does day-to-day. This part of the book provides information about some of the wide variety of jobs available in the software industry, and the different kinds of organization where you might find yourself working.

Code Download

All the code examples used in the book are available for download from github, here:

`https://github.com/simonmonk/coding_book`

You can download all the file as a ZIP archive (see Page 34).

The book's website

For errata, and further information on the book see the book's web page at: `http://simonmonk.org/coding_book`

Acknowledgements

Many thanks to Ian Huntley and Vincent Lyles for their helpful technical review and copy editing. Many thanks also to Dave, Stephen, Matthew and Linda Monk, who's feedback was very useful.

I think this book has been greatly improved by the inclusion of comic strips from CommitStrip. I'd like to thank the CommitStrip team for their permission to include the strips. Their observational humour on the software industry is very funny. I heartily recommend you to visit them at `https://www.commitstrip.com/`

Contents

Contents

_1_

Introduction

In this chapter we will go on a whirlwind tour of the software development industry and look at what someone might expect when embarking on a new career.

We will explore exactly what we mean by *coding* and what code actually looks like, as well as looking at what jobs are available in software development.

By kind permission of commitstrip.com

What is Programming or Coding?

There is no universally accepted definition that distinguishes *coding* from *programming*, but the distinction has, perhaps, come about because a lot of what goes into creating a software system involves just editing files of text that don't, in a pure sense, contain programs.

In this book we will mostly use the term *coding* to describe the activity of writing code for computer systems. When it comes to the job title of someone who does this, then *developer* is, perhaps, the most used term.

Coding is all about making a computer system do some job that we want it to do. What we want the computer to do can vary enormously. Mostly, today, we want computers to be a web server, serving a website, which we can connect to from our browser and do things like buy books, or order any number of goods and services. Behind the scenes, computer programs will be working away, making the system as a whole function.

The *front-end* user interface program (running in your browser) that you might use to buy a product online will be interacting with other programs that order more products from suppliers, create work orders to shift products from one warehouse to another, provide instructions for delivery drivers, and record that the product was actually delivered to you. These different programs will probably use different technologies, but the key thing is that someone will have written code in various programming languages to make this system work.

Computer software is one of the most complex thing that humans create. Unconstrained by the need to be physically made out of metal, nuts and bolts, computer software running on a general purpose computer can grow and grow as more features are added. This increasing complexity is one of the biggest challenges in developing software, and various strategies have been developed to try and keep things manageable.

You will hear (especially in job adverts) terms like back-end developer (databases and server things), front-end developer (mostly concerned with web sites), or full-stack developer (everything). In addition to these different areas of expertise, programmers will generally specialise in certain programming languages, building up a set of skills

By kind permission of commitstrip.com

as their careers progress.

Even if you don't want to be employed as a programmer, having the ability to program is a useful skill in our ever more technology-centred society. You may well find aspects of your work, or life that you can automate by writing a quick bit of Python.

How do you Program?

In modern programming teams, aside from meetings and general employment admin, when a developer is coding, they will have a task to be completed in front of them.

Let's invent a fairly mundane, but probably quite typical, example.

1. Introduction

The task is to change the software system (let's say its a delivery system) so that on a web page that the customer uses there is a new field, where they can specify a safe place to leave a package if they are out.

The developer will be working on their own copy of the system, usually running on their own computer (strangely, developers don't often use the word *computer*, preferring just *machine*). They may be working on the task on their own, or they may sometimes be pair-programming. If pair-programming, then they will be working as a couple – one programmer typing in new code as the other watches, offering advice and reminders.

Pair programming has been shown to offer advantages in terms of code quality, and also in programmer's skills development, but of course at a financial cost. These days, one part of the pair is often an AI (Artificial Intellegence) built into the software tool used to write the code.

The steps the developer take might typically be something like this:

1. They might start by reminding themselves of how that part of the system works – looking at the web page, the code for which they are about to change.

2. They will then find the programming code files (called *source code*) for this part of the user interface, and find the places where the changes need to be made.

3. Actually making the change will require some new code for the *where to leave the package* field, but will also need other code writing for things like validating what the user enters, and making sure that whatever is entered by the user finds its way to the backend server. This last part might actually be a separate task.

4. Often, automated tests (more coding) will be created, the tests simulate someone entering the new information and makes sure it gets stored and that it works for various different scenarios and data entered by the user. Writing the code for the tests is often more work than the actual code.

5. Once all the tests for the new code pass, and all the unit tests for the whole system pass, then the code can be *committed*

(shared with the other programmers). The programmer can then move onto their next task.

What does this Code Look Like?

This of course depends completely on the technologies being used. Indeed, for an online store example like the one from the previous section there might be a real mixture of technologies.

Here are a few fragments of code, taken from various places in this book. Please don't let their apparent complexity put you off. If you can discern a little of what they mean, then great – but all will be explained as the book progresses.

First an example of some Python to work through a list in random order. Note there is a simpler way to do this (as we will see on 85).

```python
import random
from copy import copy

list = ['a', 'b', 'c']

working_list = copy(list)
while len(working_list) > 0 :
    x = random.choice(working_list)
    print(x)
    working_list.remove(x)
```

As you can see, the code is color-coded, with key words highlighted, the choice of color has no real significance, it just serves to make the code easier to read. This color-coding or, *syntax highlighting*, is a feature offered by most code editing tools.

Here is an example from Chapter 7, where some Python code is used to configure a django web server. In this case, even though the code is Python, it is used in a descriptive manner, rather than as the procedural *do something* code of the previous example.

Much of this code (the lines prefixed with a #) are comments telling a developer what to do, rather than actual program code for the computer to perform.

```
# Quick-start development settings - unsuitable for production
# See https://docs.djangoproject.com/en/4.1/howto/deployment/checklist/

# SECURITY WARNING: keep the secret key used in production secret!
SECRET_KEY = 'django-insecure-_07dy91~njgoxqqc=_)-0ps6#k8m18&4*taq9$aqu)n*f%jfOo'

# SECURITY WARNING: don't run with debug turned on in production!
DEBUG = True

ALLOWED_HOSTS = []
```

Other types of code that you will encounter include HTML (Hyper-Text Markup Language), a fragment of which is taken from Chapter 7. This is all about displaying things on a web page.

```
<div id="vapp">
    <h1>Contacts</h1>

    <div class="list-group">
        <a v-for="contact in contacts" class="list-group-item list-group-item-action">
            <div class="d-flex w-100 justify-content-between">
                <h5 class="mb-1">{{contact.fields.first_name}} {{contact.fields.surname}}</h5>
            </div>
            <p class="mb-1">{{contact.fields.email}} {{contact.fields.dob}}</p>
        </a>
    </div>
    <div>
        <button class="btn btn-primary" v-on:click="load_items">Refresh</button>
    </div>
</div>
```

In this type of code, text is *marked-up* with *tags* that control the appearance of the interspersed text in a browser.

Also taken from Chapter 7, here is some JavaScript code used to fetch data from a web server. This code is embedded in a web page and runs on the user's browser.

In this book, we will be concentrating on Python, but we will also meet a little JavaScript (like the example below) along the way.

```
<script>
    var app = new Vue({
        el: '#vapp',
        data: {
            contacts: []
        },
        mounted: function () {
            this.load_items();
        },
        methods: {
            load_items: function () {
                const xhr = new XMLHttpRequest();
                xhr.open("GET", "/contacts/list");
                xhr.send();
                xhr.responseType = "json";
                xhr.onload = () => {
                    if (xhr.readyState == 4 && xhr.status == 200) {
                        const data = xhr.response;
                        this.contacts = data;
                    } else {
```

```
            console.log(`Error: ${xhr.status}`);
        }
    };
},
}
});
</script>
```

Can Anyone Learn to Program?

Since there are so many aspects to programming, then perhaps a better question to ask is, can anyone find a role within the software development industry. To which the answer is yes.

Let's consider that learning the core skill of writing a computer program is rather like learning any skill and so practice and persistence are the keys to success. Some people take to programming more easily than others, but the same can be said of writing or any other creative activity.

By kind permission of commitstrip.com

And here is an important concept that people fail to appreciate – and that is, that programming is first and foremost a creative activity. A computer program to play a game or sell a book is literally created from nothing more than a human brain and words. Because these words are understood and acted upon by a general purpose computing machine, then it sometimes feels like there are no practical limits. Once you know how to program, then the knowledge that you can write a program to do almost anything you want is very powerful.

Many a shy teenager has found their ability to make things happen with code to be a great boost to their confidence.

A programmer may not be very good at solving Sudoku puzzles, but they can write a program to solve as many sudoku puzzles as they like. What's more they can write a program to set sudoku puzzles. Such creativity is the ultimate in the tool-using that enables much of human progress.

Machine Learning

This idea of programming computers to do tasks reaches its peak in *machine learning*. Machine learning is all about the creation of artificial intelligences (AIs) that are often very good at specific tasks such as recognising faces or sounds or choosing things that a consumer might be interested in buying.

As the name machine *learning* implies, the creation of these artificial intelligences involves training them on huge amounts of data. This training usually involves lots of work for coders to automate this training and link the AI to regular software such as websites.

Generative AI takes the huge leap from the analytical (spotting patterns or recognising things) to the synthetic (creating new things). These AIs, such as the famous ChatGTP, learn to create things such as poems, stories, advertising copy and even visual art, music, and code itself. They do this by first absorbing vast amount of data from the internet.

The impact of AI on humanity is going to be profound, and it is by no means certain that the impact of generative AI will be completely for the good. The results of generative AI, while usually extremely plausible, are often factually incorrect, reflecting the quality of the information they were trained on in the internet.

Although generative AI is proving helpful to programmers in the detail of the programming task they are working on, it's still a long way from deciding *what* to code and, in the short and medium term, machine learning will require many human programmers.

What is a Programming Job Like?

Well, as you might imagine, this is not a question with a single answer. Programming jobs can be fantastically creative fast-moving environments, working on green-field development where you get to make all the decisions. They can also be, frankly, quite dull propping up ageing software systems that are long past their best. However, software jobs will usually be something in-between these extremes. Even dull system maintenance can often eventually leads to a grand re-write of the system using newer technologies. In any case, software folk tend to move jobs frequently, especially if they are given dull things to do all the time.

By kind permission of commitstrip.com

It's easy to see a large polished system that has been developed by hundreds of programmers over years, and think that programming is the domain of big business, and that the individual can't accomplish very much on their own. This isn't true. Many great software systems (probably most) have started out as the work of a single developer or a few friends, working up the first version of a software system. For example, the original search engine software for Google was written by Scott Hassan, Larry Page and Sergey Brin. Indeed, the first and somewhat controversial version of Facebook was created as a solo effort by Mark Zuckerberg (a self-taught programmer).

Many professional software developers also have side projects that they work on in their own time. Mostly these are for fun, but sometimes they turn into the basis for a business.

Programmers try to avoid reinventing the wheel. When you start work on a new system, you make use of things called frameworks and libraries that other programmers have created to make their and your lives easier. In essence, almost any program of note written by a programmer will actually be 90% code written by other people.

By kind permission of commitstrip.com

Developer salaries vary enormously, depending on your skills and experience as well as the sector you are working in. But, in comparison with most jobs, coding is undoubtedly well paid.

Learning the core skill of programming is fundamentally a solo activity (even in a big class). Program code must be formed in your brain and find its way, via your keyboard, into a program. This core skill can no more be a group activity that writing a fictional short-story can. However, the reality of most software development is that this is done by teams. To stretch the creative writing analogy a little, this is like a team producing a script for a TV program, with a number of creative individuals all contributing and checking each other's work to produce something great.

Over the years, the way software is created has changed. For a while the roles of designing the software and implementing it were deliberately separated. A software development team would have, on one side business analysts deciding what the system should do, and, on the other side programmers who (in theory) as skilled technicians would simply implement the ideas of the often non-programmer business analysts. For many reasons, this mostly didn't work terribly well. By necessity, there would be a Big Design Up Front (BDUF). Everything would be set in stone before the programming would actually start. At times, business analysts would ask programmers to implement things that technically wouldn't work or were stupid, and programmers would work in a very literal manner, implementing exactly what was specified, even though it was clearly wrong. What's more, the people expected to actually use the software would be so far removed from the process that when the system was delivered to them it wasn't what they needed.

It's very hard to imagine how a computer system will actually work from reading a 500 page requirements document. In any case, the user's, requirements had often changed by the time the system was finished. So the whole way of working was far from ideal.

This all changed in a revolutionary way with the extremely influential explanation of the software development process called eXtreme Programming (or XP) by Kent Beck, Ward Cunningham and others in 1999. This way of creating software, puts programmers at the center of the process, as well as ensuring that the software can evolve as it develops with constant feedback from the final user. XP has led to a whole family of so called Agile Software Development methodologies. Of these, the most popular is called SCRUM. Working in an agile software development team is generally a whole lot of fun for the programmers, and perhaps one of the biggest factors in its success is that it makes programmers happy!

Most organisations will develop their own processes and practices for software development, adopting some agile practices, while doing other things in a more traditional way.

I'm no good at Math

Computer Science started as a branch of mathematics. The core theoretical ideas in Computer Science are mathematical, with all the rigour and formality that you would expect. However, unless you are creating new programming languages, or revolutionary new concepts, you no more need to be a computer scientist to program than you need to have a degree in English to write a novel.

So, the historical relationship between computing and math, along with early use of computers for doing big sums, leaves the misleading impression that to be a programmer, you must be good at math. This just isn't true. The key mental skill is to be able to think clearly about how to implement an algorithm to achieve some goal. Programming also gives pretty instant feedback so, while learning to program, being willing to just try things in the expectation that they probably won't work is a good mind-set to have.

Careers in Software

Some jobs (lets say a doctor) very specialized. You learn very deeply about one industry or activity (fixing people). Programming jobs can be found in almost every type of business.

If you like learning new things, then programming is a great career choice. Not only will you learn new programming languages and skills, but also you will learn about other types of business as you implement computer systems to support them.

For instance, This author's programming career has taught him about fisheries data (including 3 weeks at sea), the insurance industry and even chemical engineering.

Let's Go!

In the next chapter, we will launch ourselves straight into a bit of programming. This will give you a taste of Python programming and help you decide if this is an activity that you enjoy.

Part I.

Programming Bootcamp

This part of the book is designed to give you a taste *of* and hopefully a taste *for* programming. It is fairly briskly paced, so you may find that you may need to read, try things and then revisit them after leaving some time for them to sink in. But the end result should be that you know the basics of Python programming.

By kind permission of commitstrip.com

2

Getting Started

In this chapter we are going to look at programming in its simplest and purest form. A programming language (of which there are many) is a language in the sense that it's a medium for telling a computer what you want it to do.

So, without further ado, let's experience some programming first hand and write some code.

To do this, we are going to need some tools and, most importantly a programming language. We are going to use the Python programming language, as this is currently the most used programming language. We also need a tool that will allow us to type in Python code to create our programs. For this, we will use a free piece of software called Thonny. Thonny is available for Windows, MacOS and Linux computers and is designed for learner coders. As your programming skills progress, you will probably find yourself switching to a more advanced code editor. Programmers can be kind of fussy about the tools that they use. While this is very much a matter of personal preference, turning up to your first programming job and using Thonny is the programming equivalent of turning up for a cycle race with training wheels.

Most software development tools are free. Even high-end IDEs (Integrated Development Environments) tend to be free for personal use, only requiring money to be spent once they are used in a professional setting.

Installing Thonny

A good reason for using Thonny is that it is easy to install and can install Python at the same time. Installing Thonny, and its Python language, is just like installing any other application onto your computer.

To install Thonny, point your browser at https://thonny.org/. If you just search for Thonny, make sure that any download you do comes from the official thonny.org site (Figure 2.4), or you run the risk of downloading malware.

Figure 2.1. Downloading Thonny.

Installing Thonny on Windows.

Select the download for Windows and then select the download for your computer's architecture. This will probably be the first option, something like: *Installer with 64-bit Python 3.10, requires 64-bit Windows.*

This will download an executable installer. Run this once it has been downloaded (Figure 2.2) and the installer will guide you through the process of installing Thonny. You can accept all the default answers to the installer's questions.

It will take the installer a while to copy files and set up your environment but, when it finished, you should find a new entry in your Start menu for Thonny.

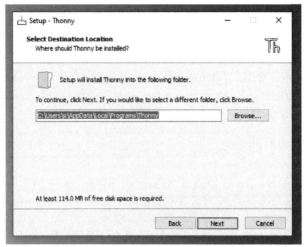

Figure 2.2. Installing Thonny in Windows.

Installing Thonny on a Mac

The Thonny installer for MacOS is a package type installer. So, having downloaded the .pkg file, open it to start the installation process (Figure 2.3).

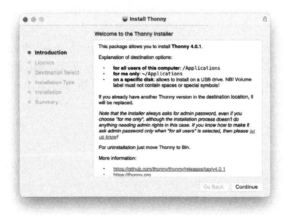

Figure 2.3. Installing Thonny in MacOS.

You can accept the default answers to all the questions that the installer asks and, once installation is complete, you will find a new application called Thonny in your applications folder.

Installing Thonny on Linux

As a Linux user, you should already be familiar with the Linux command line that you will use to install Thonny. Linux distributions generally come with Python pre-installed, and if you want Thonny to use the existing Python installation, then you can install Thonny using the command:

```
$ pip3 install thonny
```

Alternatively, you can install Thonny along with its own private version of Python using the command:

```
$ bash <(wget -O - https://thonny.org/installer-for-linux)
```

The Shell

Once you have installed Thonny, open it (Figure 2.4). Most of Thonny is made up of a large text editing area. At the bottom of the window is an area marked Shell, with an inviting looking >>> prompt. The Shell is where you can experiment with Python commands without having to write a whole program. To illustrate this, let's do a bit of arithmetic.

Click in the Shell part of the Thonny window and after the >>> prompt, type 2+2 followed by the Enter key. This will ask Python to add 2 and 2 together, and you should see the result 4.

```
>>> 2+2
4
```

Numbers

Having said that programming isn't really about math, let's start with a bit of arithmetic anyway.

Let's try out a few more examples, and get used to using the Shell. Type in the following. Note that you don't need to type in the >>>, I just use that to indicate that you should be typing in next to the

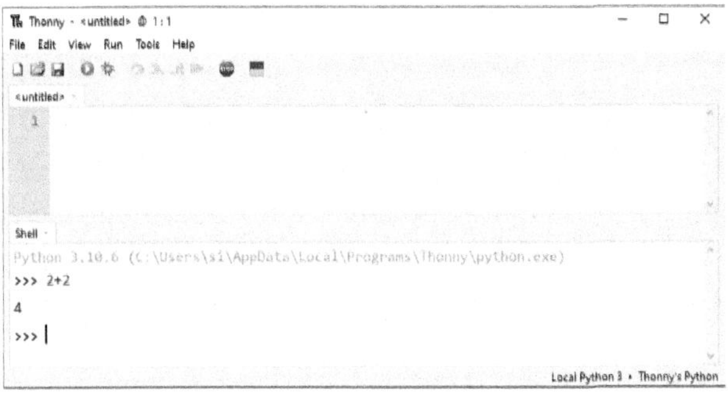

Figure 2.4. Thonny

prompt and to distinguish what you type from the response that you get from Python.

```
>>> 1 + 2 * 3
7
```

The * means multiply and Python has multiplied 2 and 3 together before adding 1, resulting in the value 7. This obeys the normal rules of arithmetic, in carrying our divisions before multiplications before additions and subtractions. If Python had just worked out the calculation left to right the result would have been 9.

If we wanted things in that order, then we could use parentheses like this:

```
>>> (1 + 2) * 3
9
```

The symbols +, -, * (multiply) and / (divide) are called operators.

Note that I have used a space character between the numbers and the + and * operators. This is not mandatory, but I think it makes the code more readable. This idea of code being readable is a big thing in programming.

So far, these numbers have all been whole numbers (called integers or ints) – there is no decimal point. If all the numbers you use in a calculation are ints and you are not using division, then the result will be an int. If you decide to use a number with a decimal place (called a float – floating point) or division in the calculation then the result will be a float. For example:

```
>>> 0.345 * 100
34.5
```

> Try typing in some more sums using both ints and floats. The Python Shell actually makes quite a useful calculator.

Naming things

So far, we could have done all this with a pocket calculator, so it's time to introduce the crucial concept in programming of a *variable*. A variable is mostly a way of giving a value a name. They are called variables because that value can change. For example, we could use a variable to represent the current sales tax rate as a percentage. The value of the tax rate might change from day to day, but it would always be called the same.

Follow along with these examples by typing the code into Thonny's Python shell.

```
>>> tax_rate = 20
```

The first thing to notice is that the name we are using has no spaces in it. Different programming languages have different rules for variable names, but, in Python, they must start with a letter and can contain numbers and the underscore character _ but no spaces or other punctuation.

The = operator is called the assignment operator, because it assigns a value to a variable (in this case 20).

Having assigned a value to this variable, Python will remember the value, at least until we restart Python by restarting Thonny. We can check this by just entering the name of the variable in the Shell:

```
>>> tax_rate
20
```

We can now use our variable in calculations, like this, calculating the tax payable on $103.50:

```
>>> 103.50 * tax_rate / 100
20.7
```

Lets say the tax rate changed to 15%, then we could assign a new value to our variable by doing this:

```
>>> tax_rate = 15
>>> 103.50 * tax_rate / 100
15.525
```

It's a bit tedious retyping the same lines into the Shell over and over again. A really useful feature of the Shell is that it remembers the past lines that you typed in, and you can recall them using the up and down cursor keys on your keyboard.

What's more, having recalled a line, you can then use the left and right cursor keys to position the cursor and modify the line, before pressing Enter to run it.

Try making some more variables and carry out arithmetic on them.

By kind permission of commitstrip.com

Strings

Aside from numbers, the most-used value for a variable is the *string*. A string is the name for a collection of characters. These can be letters or numbers or punctuation. To tell Python that something is a string you surround it with either double or single quotes. It doesn't matter which, but they must match at each end of the string. In this book, we'll mostly stick to single quotes. Here's how you would assign a string to a variable.

```
name = 'Simon'
```

You can use the + operator to add one string to the end of another (called *concatenation*) like this:

```
>>> name = 'Simon'
>>> name + ' Monk'
'Simon Monk'
>>>
```

However, if you try and add a number to a string, perhaps expecting Python to print out 'Simon 2', then you will get an error from Python.

```
>>> name + 2
Traceback (most recent call last):
  File "<stdin>", line 1, in <module>
TypeError: can only concatenate str (not "int") to str
>>>
```

Given that Python clearly knows what you are trying to do, it's a bit annoying to receive such an error message – especially when many programming languages, on encountering this situation, will automatically convert the number into a string for you.

We can fix this by using the str command that converts a number into a string, like this:

```
>>> name + str(2)
'Simon2'
```

ints floats and *strings* are called *types*. Although the int and float number types are compatible and you can mix them when doing arithmetic etc. Strings are quite different. So, even if the contents of a string look like a number, you can't actually use them as a number for arithmetic, without first converting the string to either an int or a float, as we shall see later on.

Programs

The Shell is great if you want to try out single lines of code to see what they do. However, as soon as you need to write a few lines of code to do something you need a program file. I use the phrase *program file* rather than *program* because, typically, a computer program will consist of a number of program files.

In Python program files are like any other file on your computer – like say a word processor document – but they have a *.py* on the end of the file name. The rest of the name should not have any spaces in it and follows much the same naming convention as variable names (except with *.py* on the end). Although you can use - to separate words in the file name, not all operating systems support this, and underscore (_) are generally used.

Let's create a Python program file called *test_1.py* within Thonny. Thonny will automatically start with an empty file that we can edit. This will be called *untitled*, and we just need to save the file in order for it to be given a name. To do this, click on the *Save* button in Thonny (Figure 2.6). You can also save a file from Thonny's File menu.

We are just experimenting, so it doesn't really matter where you save the file, but your Desktop is as good a place as any (Figure 2.7). Don't forget to give the file the name *test_1.py*.

So, now the file has a name and has been saved, even though it doesn't contain anything yet. Put the code below into the Thonny editor area for *test_1.py* and then click on the green triangular *play/run* button (Figure 2.8).

Figure 2.6. The Save button in Thonny.

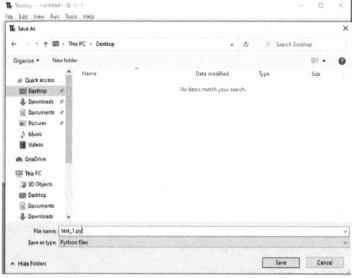

Figure 2.7. Saving a file in Thonny.

```
result = 2 + 2
print(result)
```

You should see the result 4 shown in the Shell like Figure 2.8.

When we were typing things like 2 + 2 into the Shell we saw immediate results. That's because the Shell automatically prints out the result of everything it does. This is not the case for code in a file. When using a program file, we have to use the print command to tell Python to display the thing inside its brackets (in this case the result of doing 2 + 2).

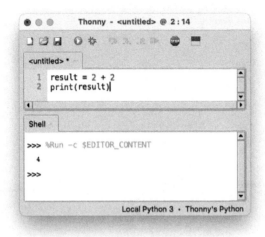

Figure 2.8. Running a program file in Thonny.

Try changing what's in the Thonny code editor area to the following to this:

```
a = 10
b = 5
result = a + b
print(result)
```

You can see the result of this in Figure 2.9.

This may only be four lines, but I think it still counts as writing your first program!

It is as if Python is reading each line of code and then performing whatever the line tells it to do. So in this example, it first assigns the value 10 to the variable a and then 5 to the variable b, then adds them together and finally prints the result.

The program is like a list of instructions to follow, one after another. If you want to save this program, then you need to remember to click the Save button. Thonny actually runs the code in the editor window, whether it's saved or not.

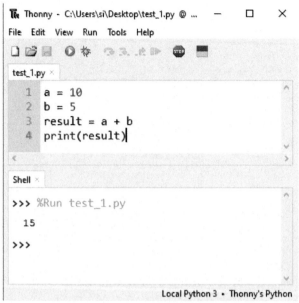

Figure 2.9. A four line program.

Try changing the variable values in the example above and rerunning the program.

Also, try saving the program, quitting Thonny and then restarting it and then make sure you can re-open the file *test1.py*.

Input and Output

We have used print to display the string 'Hello' in the Shell. Its counterpart input allows us to prompt the user to type something in. Type the following code into the Thonny editor area. However, if you want to keep the old program file, then start a new program file first by clicking on the *New* icon (top left – it looks like a sheet of paper) or from the menu, *File* and then *New*.

```python
text = input('Enter text:')
polite_text = text + ' please.'
print(polite_text)
```

You can see the result of running this in Figure 2.10.

Figure 2.10. Using the input command.

Like the print command from the earlier example, the input command has parentheses after it containing a string. The thing inside the parentheses is called a *parameter*, and here it tells Python what to display as a reminder to the user of what they should enter.

Making Decisions

Programs would be pretty inflexible if all they could do was to follow mechnically a list of instructions in order. We need a way of making decisions in our code. One way of doing this uses the word if. When you come to type in the code below, into Thonny's editor area, you will notice that when you press Enter at the end of the third line, the fourth line will automatically be indented by 4 spaces.

Python needs indentation to be consistent. Helpfully, Thonny always indents by 4 spaces.

Even if you use the TAB key, Thonny will insert 4 space characters rather than a single tab character. Some code editors will not do this and, even through a tab character may appear on the screen to indent by 4 spaces, Python does not treat them as the same thing and will give error messages if you try and run code that mixes tabs and spaces.

```
n_str = input('Enter a number:')
n = int(n_str)
if n > 10:
    print('the number is big!')
```

Try running the program above and when prompted in the Shell, enter the number 30. You should see the message displayed saying *the number is big!*. Run the program again, but enter the number 5 – this time no message should be displayed. So, now our program is doing some of the code only if a certain condition is satisfied (n is greater than 10).

Taking a closer look at the code, you can see that we start by asking the user to enter a number, and assign that number to the variable n_str. Even though we type in a number, what ends up in n_str will be a string (that's why we called it n_str rather than just n (for number). On the second line we convert that string to a number using the int command, so that we can compare the number with 10 in line below that. If we wanted the user to be able to enter numbers with a decimal point (floats) we would have to replace n = int(n_str) with n = float(n_str).

Note that a string containing a number is not the same as an actual number, so you must convert it to an int or float before you try and treat it like a number by, say, adding another number to it.

Try creating a string variable in the Shell with a value in single quotes that is a number-like string (perhaps '-123') and use int to convert it into a number.

Immediately after the if command, there must be what is called a *condition*. This condition can only ever result in a value that is either `True` or `False`. After the condition is a colon (`:`). If the condition is satisfied (`True`), then any indented lines after the `if` line will run (in this case printing a message). Indenting the lines after the `if` tells Python that those lines in a sense belong to the `if` command.

A variation on the `if` command is to follow it with an `else` command as shown here:

```
n_str = input('Enter a number:')
n = int(n_str)
if n > 10:
    print('the number is big!')
else:
    print('the number is small')
```

Run the program a few times, entering different numbers and you will see that you get different messages depending on whether the number is greater than 10 or not.

As well as `>` for greater than, you can also use `<` for less than, `<=` for less than or equal to and `>=` for greater than or equal to. You can also use `==` for exactly equal to and `!=` for not equal to. Note the double `=` sign (`==`), to distinguish comparing numbers from assigning a value to a variable. You can also use `>`, `<`, `==` etc with strings and the comparison will be by alphabetical order. You can try this out in the Shell.

```
>>> 'Abacus' > 'Calculator'
False
>>> 'Abacus' < 'Calculator'
True
>>> 'Abacus' == 'Calculator'
False
>>>
```

Notice how Python reports either `True` of `False` in response to the comparison. These values are special values called *Boolean* values.

Comparing strings is case sensitive, with all lowercase letters beaing greater than any uppercase letter. For example:

```
>>> 'a' > 'B'
True
>>> 'a' > 'b'
False
```

> Try typing lots of different comparisons into Thonny's Shell.
> What happens if you try and compare a string with a number?

As well as comparing values, if statements can also use and and or to make more complex comparisons. For example we could look for medium-sized numbers by writing something like:

```
if n > 10 and n < 20:
    print('n is medium-sized')
```

Repeating Ourselves

As well as performing some commands only when a condition is True, Python has various ways of repeating the same commands multiple times. Try out the following code and then read it through to try to work out why it prints out the numbers 1 to 10.

Listing 2.1: 02_01_counting.py

```
count = 1
while count <= 10:
    print(count)
    count = count + 1
```

Here we have a variable called count that we have given an initial value of 1. We then have a while command that is followed by a condition (rather like if). But, in this case, the condition dictates whether the while should continue running the two lines of code within it.

We would normally call the while plus the two lines (in the example above) that follow it as a *while loop*.

The first of these lines prints out the current value of count (1 the first time). The second line adds 1 to count, so that the next time around the loop, `count` will have a value of 2 that will be printed and so on until `count` is no longer less than or equal to 10 and the loop finishes and, because there is no code after the `while` loop, the whole program finishes too.

Since adding an amount to a variable is such a common thing to do, Python has a short cut for this. So, instead of writing:

```
count = count + 1
```

you can write:

```
count += 1
```

Both lines do exactly the same thing. As well as +=, you will also find -=, *= and /= that work in a similar way, but for subtraction, multiplication and division.

> Try changing the code of 02_01_counting.py so that it counts up to 1000.
> Now try changing it so that it counts to a million. It'll take a while to do this, but you can stop it by clicking on the Stop button in Thonny's toolbar. Note that you can also stop a program running by pressing CTRL-C in the Shell.
> Change the code again, so that it increases by 10 each time rather than 1

Another way of looping, particularly a fixed number of times, is to use the `for` command. This can be combined with the range command as shown below.

```
for x in range(1, 10):
    print(x)
```

Listing: 02_02_for_loop.py

Note that when you run this program you will see that only the numbers 1 to 9 are printed, not the number 10, even though range specifies 1 to 10. That is because the upper bound of range is *exclusive*. That is, the range only includes numbers up to 1 less than the upper range.

Code Download

All the code for this book is available for download. It is hosted on the *github* site, and you can either just view it there, copying code from the website and pasting it into Thonny, or you can download all the code in one go. To see the code, visit the following address in your browser:

`https://github.com/simonmonk/coding_book`

Github is just a place to store files and, you can browse the files that are organized into different folders or directories, just like you would on your computer. Clicking on the *python* link (on the left) will take you to a list of all the programs for the book, you can click on these to view the code for that program. Model answers to the exercises are provided in a folder called *exercise_solutions*.

As well as viewing the programs online, you can also download them all as a ZIP file archive by clicking on the *Code* button and then selecting *Download ZIP* from the menu that appears (see Figure 2.11).

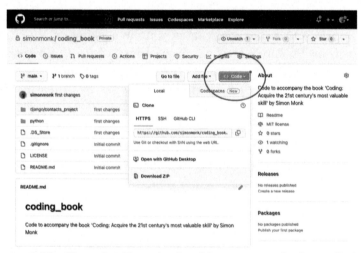

Figure 2.11. Downloading the book's source code from Github.

Once downloaded, the ZIP file can be extracted and you can then open and run the files in Thonny.

Wherever there is a code listing in the book that has a heading that names the file, that is the name of the file on Github.

Exercises

To test your knowledge on what you have learnt so far, here are some exercises. The third of these is deliberately hard, so don't worry if you need to jump to the solution with the book downloads and in Appendix B.

Exercise 2-1.

Write a program that asks the user to enter two numbers, and then display a message saying the numbers are the same only if they are the same.

You can find a solution to this exercise, as well as all the other exercises, in the downloads for this book (see Page 34) and in Appendix B.

Exercise 2-2.

Write a program that asks the user to enter a password and then compares what they entered with a `saved_password` variable containing the string `'guessme'` and print the message 'Password correct' or 'Password FAIL' depending on whether what was typed in matches or not.

Exercise 2-3

This is a real stretch, so you may find that you need to jump to the solution in the code download for the book. The problem is to write a program that prompts the user to think of a number between 1 and 99 and the program then tries to guess the number by asking if the number is greater than a certain amount. Hint: *Lookup binary chop.*

Summary

Congratulations! You have written a few simple programs and I hope you have enjoyed learning how to do this.

We started by looking at numbers and strings and then went on to look at how we could make code conditional, so that it would only run when some condition was true. We also looked at how we can make our code loop to repeat certain lines of code over and over again.

In the next chapter, we will build on these fundamentals and look at some ways of organising the data that our programs rely on.

Data Structures

So far in this book, our data (things we could assign to a variable) have been limited to two types of numbers, strings and the Boolean values of True and False.

To code, or program, is often a process of modelling some element of real life. You can break this modelling down to two things – the data involved in the system and the processing that uses that data.

So far, we have been concentrating on the processing side of things, but in this chapter, we will look at the data side of things. You will learn how to use two ways of collecting together multiple values in Python, called Lists and Dictionaries, and gradually build up your programming skills.

Lists

A Python *list* is a way of collecting together a list of values into one data structure. Most programming languages have a data type like this. They may be called *arrays*, *vectors*, or *ordered collections*. As an example, let's say we were writing a program to do something with a list of movie ttles. This could perhaps be to supply one at random from a list of movie titles, for the purposes of playing charades.

By kind permission of commitstrip.com

Creating a List

We can create such a list using square brackets to mark the start and the end of the list. Follow along with the examples below, typing them into the Shell.

```
titles = ['Jaws', 'The Godfather', 'Baby Driver', 'Inception']
```

Instead of our variable having a single value, `titles` has a list of values as its value. Notice how a list is indicated by an [and an] (square brackets) enclosing the *elements* of the list. In this case each element is a string. Notice that there is a comma between each *item* or *element*. In this example, we have used strings as the values but, actually, you can use numbers or Boolean (True/False) values or even other lists as elements of a list. You can ask Python to print the list like this:

```
>>> print(titles)
['Jaws', 'The Godfather', 'Baby Driver', 'Inception']
>>>
```

Accessing Elements of a List

You can fetch an item from a list by its position (its index) in a list like this:

```
>>> titles[2]
'Baby Driver'
>>>
```

You might be wondering why, when we asked for item 2 from the list, we actually got the third item in the list. The reason for this is that list positions start at 0 rather than 1. So if we ask for `titles[0]` we will get 'Jaws'. You can also replace particular elements of a list like this:

```
>>> titles[0] = 'Mad Max'
>>> titles
['Mad Max', 'The Godfather', 'Baby Driver', 'Inception']
>>>
```

If you try and access an element of the list that is beyond the end of the list, you will get an error:

```
>>> titles[5]
Traceback (most recent call last):
  File "<stdin>", line 1, in <module>
IndexError: list index out of range
>>>
```

In Chapter 6 we will learn more about error messages like this and how to deal with them in our code. But, generally speaking, it's better to write code that avoids causing the errors in the first place.

To illustrate how we might do this, let's write a program to ask the user for a number, and then print the movie title at that position. We'll put the code in a `while` loop that continues forever, so that we don't have to keep running the program multiple times. Here is a first version of the code.

```
titles = ['Jaws', 'The Godfather', 'Baby Driver', 'Inception']

while True:
    index_str = input('Enter index number: ')
    index = int(index_str)
    print(titles[index])
```

There are a few things here that we should explain about the code. First of all the `while` loop. This has a condition of just `True`. That means that the `while` loop will continue forever – unless we quit the program or, as we shall see in a moment, we get an error.

The other new thing is that the last line of the code has a `print` command that has as its parameter `titles[index]`. That is, we haven't put the result of doing `titles[index]` into a separate variable and then printed it (we could if we wanted) but rather we have used actual code as the parameter to `print` rather than just a variable name.

Try running the program, at first entering 0 and then entering 7, as shown below.

```
Enter index number: 0
Jaws
Enter index number: 7
Traceback (most recent call last):
  File "03_01_list_access.py", line 6, in <module>
    print(titles[index])
IndexError: list index out of range
```

Remember that the positions in the list start at 0.

As you can see, because our list only has 4 elements, the maximum allowed index value is 3. Let's now modify the program so that, before using the value of `index`, it first checks that it's in the allowed range of values, using an `if` command.

Listing: 03_01_list_access.py

```
titles = ['Jaws', 'The Godfather', 'Baby Driver', 'Inception']
num_titles = len(titles)

while True:
    index_str = input('Enter index number: ')
    index = int(index_str)
```

```
if index >= 0 and index < num_titles:
    print(titles[index])
else:
    print('Index must be between 0 and ' + str(num_titles - 1))
```

You can see the final version of this program in the file *03_01_list_access.py*. The first thing to notice is the second line of the program:

```
num_titles = len(titles)
```

The len command returns the length of a list.

> The len command also works on strings. Try typing len('abc') in the Shell. You should get the answer 3 (3 characters in the string).

Now, in our while loop, you can see that we have an if/else statement that checks that the index is greater than or equal to 0 and less than whatever the length of the list is before trying to access that element.

Adding to and Removing from Lists

You can add items to a list using the append command, like this:

```
>>> titles = ['Jaws', 'The Godfather', 'Baby Driver', 'Inception']
>>> titles.append('ET')
>>> titles
['Jaws', 'The Godfather', 'Baby Driver', 'Inception', 'ET']
>>>
```

Notice how the append command is used. It goes straight after the name of the list variable (titles) and is separated it from it by a dot. This is quite different to how we found the length of the list by writing len(titles). These two styles are a result of the evolution of the Python language and can be confusing at first.

The len way of doing things is called a *function* and the append way is called a *method*. This dot notation (part of object-orientation) will be explained properly in Chapter 5.

Removing items from a list uses the delightfully named pop method.

This takes as its parameter, the index of the list element to be removed.

```
>>> titles = ['Jaws', 'The Godfather', 'Baby Driver', 'Inception']
>>> titles.pop(0)
'Jaws'
>>> titles
['The Godfather', 'Baby Driver', 'Inception', 'ET']
>>>
```

Iterating over Lists

When you have a list like our list of movie titles, it is very common to want to do something to each element of the list. We could do this with a `while` loop and an `index` variable that we kept incrementing as the code in *03_02_list_iterating_while.py* below.

Listing: 03_02_list_iterating_while.py

```
titles = ['Jaws', 'The Godfather', 'Baby Driver', 'Inception']

index = 0

while index < len(titles):
    print(titles[index])
    index += 1
```

This will produce output in the Shell like this:

```
Jaws
The Godfather
Baby Driver
Inception
```

Notice how each element of the list printed on a line of its own.

Because iterating over lists is such a common thing to do, even though Python has a special command for this called `for`. The program file *03_03_list_iterating_for.py* does exactly the same thing as the previous program, but looks a bit neater and uses less lines of code.

```
titles = ['Jaws', 'The Godfather', 'Baby Driver', 'Inception']

for title in titles:
    print(title)
```

The `for` command is really a `for/in` command. Immediately after `for` is the name of a new variable (in this case `title`) that will be assigned to each of the titles in turn. After `in` the list to be iterated over is specified (`titles`).

Sorting and Filtering

Say we want to put our list into alphabetical order. Well, we can do that using the `sort` method:

```
>>> titles = ['Jaws', 'The Godfather', 'Baby Driver', 'Inception']
>>> titles.sort()
>>> titles
['Baby Driver', 'Inception', 'Jaws', 'The Godfather']
```

If, having sorted our list of movies, we for some reason wanted them in descending alphabetical order we could use the `reverse` method to reverse the order of the list.

```
>>> titles.reverse()
>>> titles
['The Godfather', 'Jaws', 'Inception', 'Baby Driver']
```

We will be using lists throughout this book, but I think we've covered enough to get us started. You might like to try Exercise 3-1 at the end of this chapter before moving on to look at another type of data structure called dictionaries.

Dictionaries

In a list elements are accessed by their position, whereas in a dictionary, elements are accessed by a *key*. So, to continue our movie example, a dictionary might be used to store a number of features of a particular movie.

Follow along with the examples by typing the code into Thonny's Shell.

```
>>> movie = { 'title':'Jaws', 'director':'Steven Spielberg', 'duration': 124 }
```

Each pair in the dictionary is called a key/value pair. The *key* is used to look up the *value*. Whereas a list uses square brackets to enclose its contents, dictionaries use *curly braces* - {}.

Accessing a Dictionary

The code above creates a new dictionary with three keys, *title*, *director* and *duration*, representing information about a particular movie. We can then access the value for a particular key using the same square bracket syntax as we did for lists, but instead of putting an index number inside the square brackets, we put the key. So to find the title, we would use:

```
>>> movie['title']
'Jaws'
```

The value of an element of a dictionary can be any type you want. So, in this example, `title` and `director` are strings, but `duration` is a number (running time in minutes).

Just like lists, you can also set the value at a particular key as follows. In this example, perhaps you need to change the title to that of a different movie.

```
>>> movie['title'] = 'Jaws 2'
>>> movie
{'title': 'Jaws 2', 'director': 'Steven Spielberg', 'duration': 124}
```

To add new key value pair elements to the dictionary just specify a new key. So to add a new attribute year to the dictionary, you can just do this:

```
>>> movie['year'] = 1978
```

A List of Dictionaries

In the movies dictionary example that we are developing there is only one movie. For multiple movies, we can put a number of dictionaries in a list. You probably won't want to type this into the Shell (as its quite a lot to type), but you can find it at the top of the file *03_04_list_dict.py*.

```
movies = [
    { 'title':'Jaws', 'director':'Steven Spielberg', 'duration': 124 },
    { 'title':'The Godfather', 'director':'Francis Ford Coppola,', 'duration': 175 },
    { 'title':'Baby Driver', 'director':'Edgar Wright', 'duration': 115 }
]
```

Notice that we have put each dictionary in the list on a line of its own. Remember to put a comma at the end of each dictionary except the last one in the list.

You can also add more spacing to make it easier to read the code and check that you have the right numbers of opening and closing curly braces, putting each of the dictionary elements on a line of its own like this:

```
movies = [
    {
        'title':'Jaws',
        'director':'Steven Spielberg',
        'duration': 124
    },
    {
        'title':'The Godfather',
        'director':'Francis Ford Coppola,',
        'duration': 175
    },
    {
        'title':'Baby Driver',
        'director':'Edgar Wright',
        'duration': 115
    },
]
```

The indentation is critical here, with each dictionary element indented the same amount. Thonny will help you with this, indenting by 4 positions whenever you press the TAB key. It will also automatically indent and put the cursor in the right position when you start a new line after a line that ends in a : as we have seen with earlier examples on `while` and `for`.

To read through each element of the list and display just the title, we can use `for`/`in`. You can find this code in *03_04_list_dict.py*.

Listing: 03_04_list_dict.py

```
for movie in movies:
    print(movie['title'])
```

This will produce output in the Shell like this:

```
Jaws
The Godfather
Baby Driver
```

We can filter our lists. For example, what if we wanted to select films less than two hours long (because we didn't have much time to watch a movie). One way we could do this is to start an empty list, then for each of the movie titles in turn, if the duration is greater than 2 hours (120 minutes) add it to the new list.

What we have done here is thought up an algorithm to enable us to filter the list of movies. The program below (*03_05_filter.py*) does this.

Listing: 03_05_filter.py

```
short_movies = []

for movie in movies:
    if movie['duration'] < 120:
        short_movies.append(movie)

print(short_movies)
```

The [] on the first line looks a bit odd, but this is just the way that you tell Python to create an empty list. This may sound like a strange thing to do, but even though the list starts empty, new items will be added to it to build up the list of short films.

Tuples

Python actually has a second list-like type called a *tuple*. Whereas a list uses square brackets, a tuple uses round, like this:

```
>>> tuple = (1, 'linda', 23)
>>> tuple[1]
'linda'
```

Many of the things that you can do with a list, you can also do with a tuple. But the really big difference between a tuple and a list is that a tuple is *immutable* – that is, you cannot change it once it's been created. You cannot add or remove elements, or change any of the items in the tuple.

Exercises

Here are a few exercises for you to test your knowledge of data structures. You can find solutions to these exercises in the folder *exercise_solutions* in the download for this book and in Appendix B.

Exercise 3-1.

Write a short program that starts with an empty list then uses a while loop and the input command to keep prompting the user to enter a new movie title. Each time a new title is added, the list of titles should be printed. For a bonus, the program should exit if the title added is blank (its length is 0). Hint: the break command jumps out of a loop.

Exercise 3-2.

Starting with the code in *03_04_list_dict.py*, modify the program so that the movie's duration is printed after the movie title in parentheses.

Exercise 3-3.

Write a pointless program that puts all the numbers between 1 and 10,000,000 into a list. How long does it take for the program to run on your computer?

Summary

In this chapter, we have learnt some of the basics of using lists and dictionaries. In later chapters, we will build on this foundation, as there is a lot more to learn about these types of data structure.

In Chapter 7, we will see how lists of dictionaries can be a very handy way of representing data extracted from a database.

Functions

When you are writing small programs, like the ones we have been writing so far, they only really perform one job, so it's fairly easy to see what they are trying to achieve. As programs get larger then things get more complicated and it becomes necessary to break up your programs into units called *functions*. When we get even further into programming, we will look at even better ways of structuring our programs using classes and modules in Chapter 6.

By kind permission of commitstrip.com

Many of the things that I have been referring to as *commands* are actually *functions* built into Python. Examples of this are - `input`, `str` and `print`. As well as built-in functions, we can create our own functions.

The definitive guide to the Python language and modules can be found here: `https://docs.python.org/3/library/index.html`. It can be useful and informative to browse this area, just to get a feel for what Python can do.

When it comes to finding out how to do something specific in Python, the chances are, you won't be the first person to want to know how to do this, and an Internet search will find you the answer. The *stackexchange.com* website often provides the best answers.

You can also ask a generative AI, such as ChatGTP, how to do things or even how to write code for you. The results of this can be really quite impressive.

The biggest problem in software development, of any sort, is managing complexity. The *best* developers write software that is easy to look at and understand and requires very little in the way of extra explanation. Functions are a key tool in creating easy to understand programs that can be changed without difficulty.

Functions

A function is a little like a program within a program. We can use it to wrap up some little thing that we want to do. A function, that we define, can be called (run) from anywhere in our program, and will contain its own variables and its own list of commands. When the commands have been run we will return to just after wherever it was in the code that we called the function from in the first place.

As an example, let's make a function that makes strings more polite by adding the word 'please' to the end of the string. The function will need to know the string to be made polite, and this is called a *parameter* to the function. You may remember we did something similar without using a function on page 28. The difference here is that we are wrapping up the code to do this into a function that we can use again and again – we will call this function `make_polite`. Having created such a function, then we can use it from anywhere within our code.

Load the file below, or type it into a new editor window. Run it to see what happens.

Listing: 04_01_polite_function.py

```
def make_polite(sentence):
  polite_sentence = sentence + ' please'
  return polite_sentence

print(make_polite('Pass the salt'))
```

The function starts with the keyword `def`, short for define. This is followed by the name of the function, that follows the same naming rules and conventions as variables. After that come the parameters inside parentheses and separated by commas (if there are more than one). The first line must end with a colon to indicate that any lines below that are indented (by 4 spaces) and should be treated as part of the function.

You can think of *parameters* as a way of giving extra information to the function about what you want it to do. In this case, telling the function what it is that we want to make polite.

Inside the function, we are using a new variable called `polite_sentence` that takes the *parameter* passed in to the function and adds `'please'` to it. This variable can only be used from inside the function. This may seem like a rather arbitrary restriction but, by limiting the scope of the variable to inside the function, it helps to prevent code getting complicated and difficult to follow. You don't need to worry about what else might be altering the value of variable that is local to a function because such interactions are not allowed. In other words, the function is self-contained.

The last line of the function is a `return` command. This specifies what value the function should give back to the code that called it. In this case, what is returned is the value of the variable `polite_sentence`.

To use the function, we just specify its name and supply it with the appropriate arguments in the Shell – for example:

```
>>> make_polite('Pass the salt')
Pass the salt please
```

A really key point to understand here is the difference between *defining* a function and *calling* a function. When we define a function using def the code inside that function will not be run unless we later *call* or *invoke* that function, as we did in *04_01_polite_function.py*. To reinforce this point, try deleting the line:

```
print(make_polite('Pass the salt'))
```

from *04_01_polite_function.py* and run it again. You should not see any message printed out. We have just defined a function telling it how to make things polite, without actually telling it to make anything polite.

A return value is not mandatory and some functions will just do something rather than calculate something. So, for example, we could write a rather pointless function that prints 'Hello' a specified number of times:

Listing: 04_02_hello_n.py

```
def say_hello(n):
  for x in range(0, n):
    print('Hello')

say_hello(5)
```

Global and Local Variables

Most of the variables we have met so far in this book are called *global* variables. That is, they are accessible from anywhere within the program. Functions can contain *local* variables (like polite_sentence in 04_01_polite_function.py) that are only accessible by other code within the same function.

In *04_02_hello_n.py* the parameter n is a *local* variable. It cannot be accessed from anywhere except inside the say_hello function. Since n is a local variable there is no reason why we can't use the name n for other local variables in different functions, as each n will be a distinct and separate variable.

We can see the local and global variables in action by running the example *04_03 local_global.py* (Figure 4.2).

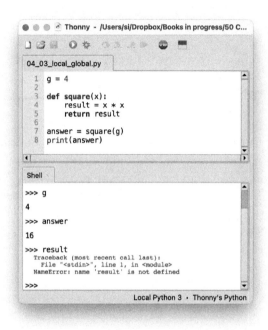

Figure 4.2. Local and global variables.

We have defined a function called `square` that takes a parameter x, multiplies it by itself and then returns the `result`. Try running the program and then in the Shell, see what happens when you try and access the various variables used, as shown in Figure 4.2.

- g is accessible (its a global)

- answer is accessible (its also a global)

- result gives an error, as does the parameter x

result and x give errors because the Shell only has access to global variables and result and x are only accessible from within the function square itself.

Whether a variable is *local* or *global* is called the *scope* of the variable.

As your programs get bigger and divided into more and more functions, you will find that you will hardly need to use global variables at all.

Parameters

The function examples so far (`make_polite`, `say_hello` and `square`) have only taken a single parameter contained in parentheses. If your function needs more than one parameter, then you can add them inside the parentheses, separated by commas. For example, if we wanted to write a function that printed a message supplied to it rather than always *hello*, we could write a function called `say_message` as shown in 04_04_multi_params.py

Listing: 04_04_multi_params.py

```
def say_message(message, num_times):
    for x in range(0, num_times):
        print(message)

say_message('Ciao', 5)
```

When you run this, you will see the message *Ciao* printed out 5 times.

When you have a function like this with multiple parameters, it can be hard to remember which parameter is which. For example, does the number of times come first or the message. It would also be handy if parameters could have default values. For example, if `num_times` were not specified when the function `say_message` was called, it would be good if it defaulted to just printing the message once. Python has a neat way of doing this, as shown in 04_05_named_params.py.

```
def say_message(message, num_times=1):
    for x in range(0, num_times):
        print(message)

say_message('once')
say_message('twice', 2)
say_message('thrice', num_times=3)
```

The first call to say_message will default to printing *once* one time, since you can miss out a parameter if a default is supplied. The second call to say_message is, if you like, a standard call to the function, and the third call uses num_times as a named variable.

Note that the *named* parameters must all come after all the normal *positional* parameters.

Comments

Comments help someone looking at the code (often a future you) to better understand what is going on.

You can add comments to your code, and they will have no effect on how the program runs. They are just remarks about the code to serve as a reminder.

Python uses the # symbol to indicate the start of a comment and will ignore anything after that until the end of the line.

We could add some explanation to our code *04_05_named_params.py*.

```
say_message('once') # illustrates default parameters
say_message('twice', 2)
say_message('thrice', num_times=3) # named parameter
```

The other place that comments can be useful is at the start of a program file, to explain what the program files does. You will also often things like the author of the code in such comments.

Comments are useful, but commenting obvious code has no benefit. For example a comment like the one below, serves no useful purpose.

```
x += 1 # Add 1 to x
```

If you want to write a multi-line comment without having to put a # at the start of each line, you can use a Python multi-line string that uses triple quote marks at the start and end like this:

```
"""
This is a
Multi-line comment
"""
```

Personally, I think it's better to stick to using # on every line of comment.

Tic-Tac-Toe

The game of Tic-Tac-Toe (or noughts and crosses if you are British), is a simple game played on a grid of 9 squares. Two players take turns to put either an *X* or an *O* on a free square and if a player can get a row of three of their symbols, either horizontally, vertically or diagonally, they are the winner.

This can be a good example of programming with more complexity that warrants a program being broken down into functions.

As anyone who has tried to learn a foreign language knows, it's very much easier to read and understand things than it is to write something, so do not worry if you cannot anticipate the way this game code develops. In any case, another programmer might do it quite differently.

Data Structure

The first thing we are going to need is a way of representing the playing grid. We need 9 locations and for each location, we need to know whether it's empty, contains an x or contains an o. There are many ways we could represent this, and there is no one right answer. Ask three developers and you'll probably get three different ways of doing this. We could use a list of lists, with each element of the list being a single string character of '.' (empty), 'x' or 'o'. This would look like this:

```
board = [
    ['x', 'o', 'o'],
    ['.', 'x', '.'],
    ['.', '.', '.']
    ]
```

We could then use a coordinate system of row and column to retrieve or alter the board. So, the bottom right corner of the board could be changed to an x (to win) by doing:

```
board[2][2] = 'x'
```

An alternative is to use a single list containing the 9 positions like this:

```
board = ['.', '.', '.',
         '.', '.', '.',
         '.', '.', '.']
```

We can still draw the playing board as a 3x3 grid of squares, but when we want to identify one of the squares of the grid, we can just use a single index position rather than having to supply (or calculate) the row and column position.

You will see why we represent each empty square with a '.' as the game develops.

Displaying the Board

Let's use this last data structure, and write a function to display the current state of the playing board. It will also display a key giving each square a number that the player to use to make their next move.

Listing: 04_06_xo_1.py

```
def show_board():
    print(board[0] + board[1] + board[2] + '  123')
    print(board[3] + board[4] + board[5] + '  456')
    print(board[6] + board[7] + board[8] + '  789')
```

4. Functions

When you run the program you should see the empty board displayed like this.

```
>>> %Run 04_06_xo_1.py
... 123
... 456
... 789
```

As well as printing the state of the playing board (in this case nine empty squares), we have also printed the numbers 1 to 9 in a grid, so that a player can pick one of those numbers for their move. We have used the human convention of numbering the squares 1 to 9 rather than 0 to 8. This will mean that we will need to subtract 1 from what the player enters to get the list index for the board square.

Taking Turns

We need a variable to tell the program whether it's o's turn or x's turn. We can call this variable `turn` and initialize it to x (assuming x starts). We can now also add a `while` loop so that each player can take a turn adding to the `board`.

Listing: 04_07_xo_2

```
board = ['.', '.', '.',
         '.', '.', '.',
         '.', '.', '.']

turn = 'x'

def show_board():
    print(board[0] + board[1] + board[2] + ' 123')
    print(board[3] + board[4] + board[5] + ' 456')
    print(board[6] + board[7] + board[8] + ' 789')

show_board()

while True:
    position_str = input('Move for ' + turn + ' :')
    position = int(position_str)
    board[position - 1] = turn
    show_board()
    if turn == 'x':
```

```
            turn = 'o'
    else:
            turn = 'x'
```

Inside the `while` loop, the user is prompted to enter the position (1 to 9) where they want to place their mark. This has to be converted from a string to an `int` and then 1 is subtracted from it to make the index to the board list.

The next piece of logic, in the form of an `if` command, swaps the turn from x to o and vice versa, ready for the next time around the loop.

Try running the program and you will find that you can play a game, but there is no checking for winners or anything to prevent one player over-writing another player's move.

Checking for Winners

The condition for someone winning the game is that there is a row of xs or os. To test for this, we need a data structure to describe the possible winning lines, including diagonals.

There are three winning row lines, three column lines and two diagonal lines.

> Before I suggest a data structure for this, try to think how you might represent the winning lines on a Tic-Tac-Toe board. Start by thinking about how you would represent one line, and then how you would represent the collection of lines.

One way to represent this is to have a list of lists, the inner lists being sets of three indices in board that make up a line. The index positions for the grid are shown in Figure 4.3, for easy reference when working out the lines.

Here's the list of winning lines. Note that I have used a # comment next to the different types of lines (horizontal, vertical and diagonal) to make the code easier to follow.

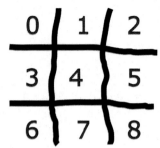

Figure 4.3. Tic-Tac-Toe index positions

```
winning_lines = [[0, 1, 2], [3, 4, 5], [6, 7, 8], # horizontal
        [0, 3, 6], [1, 4, 7], [2, 5, 8], # vertical
        [0, 4, 8], [2, 4, 6]]          # diagonal
```

We can check to see if anyone has won, by looking at each line in the list winning_lines in turn and if the contents of the board at each three positions are the same, and an o or an x, then someone has won. Let's do this with a function called check_winner that returns either . (no winner) or x or o.

```
def check_winner():
    winner = '.' # no one
    for line in winning_lines:
        if board[line[0]] == board[line[1]] == board[line[2]]:
            winner = board[line[0]] # all the same, any will do
            break
    return winner
```

The check_winner function uses a local variable called winner, that it will eventually return whether there is a winner or not. This is initialised to the string '.' (no winner).

The function then looks at each possible winning line in turn and, if the squares on each of the line indices is the same (could be 'x', 'o' or '.' the winner variable is set to whatever mark is occupying the first square in the line. We used the first (board[line[0]]) but we could use any, because they are all the same. Finally there is a break command to jump out of the loop, because we have found a winner.

This function is quite hard to follow. Take some time to work through this code in your head, imagining what it would do for various playing boards.

There is a flaw in the logic of this function, that we will look at in Exercise 4-4. Top marks if you can spot it now.

Let's now combine this with some more code in the `while` loop to check for a winner. The full listing can be found in *04_08_xo_3.py*.

Listing: 04_08_xo_3.py

```
board = ['.', '.', '.',
         '.', '.', '.',
         '.', '.', '.']

turn = 'x'

winning_lines = [[0, 1, 2], [3, 4, 5], [6, 7, 8], # horizontal
        [0, 3, 6], [1, 4, 7], [2, 5, 8], # vertical
        [0, 4, 8], [2, 4, 6]]            # diagonal

def show_board():
    print(board[0] + board[1] + board[2] + ' 123')
    print(board[3] + board[4] + board[5] + ' 456')
    print(board[6] + board[7] + board[8] + ' 789')

def check_winner():
    winner = '.' # no one
    for line in winning_lines:
        if board[line[0]] == board[line[1]] == board[line[2]]:
            winner = board[line[0]]
            break
    return winner

show_board()

while True:
    position_str = input('Move for ' + turn + ' :')
    position = int(position_str)
    board[position - 1] = turn
    show_board()
    winner = check_winner()
    if winner != '.':
        print(winner + ' wins!')
        break
    if turn == 'x':
        turn = 'o'
    else:
        turn = 'x'
```

Try playing the game, and if you contrive for one side to win, you should see something like the following in the Shell.

```
... 123
... 456
... 789
Move for x :1
x.. 123
... 456
... 789
Move for o :5
x.. 123
.o. 456
... 789
Move for x :2
xx. 123
.o. 456
... 789
Move for o :7
xx. 123
.o. 456
o.. 789
Move for x :3
xxx 123
.o. 456
o.. 789
x wins!
>>>
```

Move Checking

As the program currently stands, there is nothing to stop one player overwriting the moves of the other. We can fix this, by only allowing a player to pick an unoccupied square on which to put their mark.

This is the code from the `while` loop that we currently use to get the user to pick a square.

```
position_str = input('Move for ' + turn + ' :')
position = int(position_str)
board[position - 1] = turn
```

These lines of code can be moved into a function of their own, into which we can add the checking for move legality that we want to do.

> When programmers do something like this they call it *refactoring*. Refactoring code is a good thing, as it helps keep the code neat and easy to follow.

We will refactor the code first and then add the new feature. This results in those 3 lines above in the while loop being replaced by a call to a function called get_move, and moving those three lines into the get_move function. For brevity, just the new function and the revised while loop are listed below. (you can find the full listing in *04_09_xo_4.py*).

```python
def get_move():
    position_str = input('Move for ' + turn + ' :')
    position = int(position_str)
    board[position - 1] = turn
```

```python
while True:
    get_move()
    show_board()
    winner = check_winner()
    if  winner != '.':
        print(winner + ' wins!')
        break
    if turn == 'x':
        turn = 'o'
    else:
        turn = 'x'
```

We now need to make the game ensure that only empty squares can be chosen for a move. A nice way to do this is to write a new function called allowed_moves that returns a list of the unoccupied squares on the board. We can also use this function to see if the game has ended in a tie. This will be the case if the list returned is empty (no empty squares available). Here is the new function.

```
def allowed_moves():
    moves = []
    for move in range(1, 10):
        if board[move-1] == '.':
            moves.append(move)
    return moves
```

The `allowed_moves` function starts with an empty list, and then moves over every position on the board, adding it to the list if it's currently empty (has a . in it). Finally, it returns the list.

Let's change the way `get_move` works so that, rather than actually adding an o or an x to the board, it returns either the checked legal position for placing an x or an o, or it returns a -1 (to indicate a tie).

```
def get_move():
    position = -1 # un-chosen / no move available
    moves = allowed_moves()
    if len(moves) > 0:
        while position == -1:
            p_str = input('Move for ' + turn + str(moves) + ' :')
            p = int(p_str)
            if p in moves:
                position = p
    return position
```

We start by setting a `position` variable to -1. This variable holds the value that the function will eventually return. This is set to -1 rather than a legal position of the board (between 1 and 9) so that we can use that special value of -1 to indicate a tie.

The `allowed_moves` function is then called and the value assigned to the `moves` variable. If there are more than 0 possible moves, then we have a `while` loop where the player can keep typing positions until a legal position is supplied. We can also change the prompt for the input to include the possible legal moves. Note the use of the `str` function to convert the list into a string.

The separate variable `p` is used to capture the position temporarily until a legal one is found using the line:

```
if p in moves:
```

The in command is a useful way to check if something is in a list. In this case the move requested p is in the list of legal moves.

We now need to change the main while loop, so that it uses the new return value of get_move both to check for a tie and place an x or o. Here is the full listing:

Listing: 04_10_xo_5.py

```
board = ['.', '.', '.',
         '.', '.', '.',
         '.', '.', '.']

turn = 'x'

winning_lines = [[0, 1, 2], [3, 4, 5], [6, 7, 8], # horizontal
        [0, 3, 6], [1, 4, 7], [2, 5, 8], # vertical
        [0, 4, 8], [2, 4, 6]]            # diagonal

def show_board():
    print(board[0] + board[1] + board[2] + ' 123')
    print(board[3] + board[4] + board[5] + ' 456')
    print(board[6] + board[7] + board[8] + ' 789')

def check_winner():
    winner = '.' # no one
    for line in winning_lines:
        if board[line[0]] == board[line[1]] == board[line[2]]:
            winner = board[line[0]]
            break
    return winner

def allowed_moves():
    moves = []
    for move in range(1, 10):
        if board[move-1] == '.':
            moves.append(move)
    return moves

def get_move():
    position = -1 # un-chosen / no move available
    moves = allowed_moves()
    if len(moves) > 0:
        while position == -1:
            p_str = input('Move for ' + turn + str(moves) + ' :')
            p = int(p_str)
            if p in moves:
                position = p
    return position
```

65

```
show_board()

while True:
    position = get_move()
    if position == -1:
        print("Its a tie")
        break
    else:
        board[position-1] = turn
    show_board()
    winner = check_winner()
    if winner != '.':
        print(winner + ' wins!')
        break
    if turn == 'x':
        turn = 'o'
    else:
        turn = 'x'
```

Now when you run the program, you should find that it's pretty complete – enforcing only legal moves and checking for the end of the game.

```
>>> %Run 04_10_xo_5.py
... 123
... 456
... 789
Move for x[1, 2, 3, 4, 5, 6, 7, 8, 9] :1
x.. 123
... 456
... 789
Move for o[2, 3, 4, 5, 6, 7, 8, 9] :4
x.. 123
o.. 456
... 789
Move for x[2, 3, 5, 6, 7, 8, 9] :5
x.. 123
ox. 456
... 789
Move for o[2, 3, 6, 7, 8, 9] :9
x.. 123
ox. 456
..o 789
Move for x[2, 3, 6, 7, 8] :3
x.x 123
ox. 456
..o 789
```

```
Move for o[2, 6, 7, 8] :2
xox 123
ox. 456
..o 789
Move for x[6, 7, 8] :7
xox 123
ox. 456
x.o 789
x wins!
```

If you want to keep working on this game, you will find some exercises at the end of the chapter that improve the game further.

Using a Module

Although we will look at modules in a lot more detail in Chapter 5, let's take an early look here.

Python separates some sets of functions into separate modules that can be imported into Python when you need them. For example, random numbers are not a core part of Python. As with many features of Python it is readily available, but you have to *import* it from a *module*. Python has modules bundled with it to do all sorts of things, from accessing databases, using math functions, or even machine learning. Many of these are automatically included when you install Python, but others have to be installed separately.

Random numbers are included automatically, so all we need to do to be able to use them is to use the `import` command. Here is an example, that you can try out in the Shell or run as a program:

Listing: 04_11_dice.py

```
>>> import random
>>> x = random.randint(1, 6)
>>> print(x)
```

Try running the program and you will see that, each time, you get a number between 1 and 6 generated by `random.randint`.

If you try Exercise 4-3, you will need to use the `random` module. In particular, you will want to use the choice function as illustrated in

04_12_choice.py.

Listing: 04_12_choice.py

```
import random

fruit = ['apple', 'banana', 'pear', 'strawberry']

print(random.choice(fruit))
```

Exercises

The following exercises build on the Tic-Tac-Toe example. You can find model solutions in the *exercise_solutions* section of the book's downloads and in Appendix B.

It's important to remember that there is no one correct solution to the exercises – and if you find a different way of solving the exercise, that works, that's fine.

Exercise 4-1

Improve the appearance of the Tic-Tac-Toe board by drawing a bar between each position on the board and a line of underscores between each row.

Exercise 4-2

Change Tic-Tac-Toe so that you play against the machine. The human player x starts first, and the machine playing o picks a free square at random.

Exercise 4-3

Improve the automatic play so that if there is a winning move it is taken. Also, if there is a move that blocks x from winning, then take that move – otherwise pick a move at random.

Exercise 4-4

If you feel slightly uneasy about the function `check_winner`, then that's because it has a bug in it. Take a moment to work through it carefully, thinking about what happens if it finds a row of `'.'` before it finds a row of `'x'` or `'o'` on the board. There is an improved version of the function and explanation in the example answer for this exercise.

Summary

In this chapter we have looked at how we can keep our programs manageable by breaking them down into functions. We have also made our first sizeable example program, in the form of a tic-tac-toe game that plays against the user.

We have taken a big cognitive leap in this chapter, moving from very simple code examples into a proper program. You may find it useful to revisit this chapter and try to anticipate some of the design decisions made while the Tic-Tac-Toe game was being written. You may even like to try to write the game from scratch without reference to the book.

In Chapter 5 we will learn more about how to use modules, as well as learning about the key programming concept of object-orientation.

5

Modules and Object Orientation

In this chapter we will look in more detail at modules and also introduce and explain the idea of object-orientation. This will help us in Chapter 7, when we come to use the django web framework.

However, if you are really getting into Python all this will be of interest but, if you are more interested in an overview of programming, then you can probably jump ahead to Chapter 7, where we start to look at the more realistic example of full-stack web development (database to browser).

Importing Modules

Python includes lots of ready-made functions for us to use in our programs. If every ready-made function were immediately available to us, then there would be a real risk that we might accidentally decide to make our own function with the same name as an existing function. If there are two functions with the same name, how will Python know which one to use?

Lets find out, by defining our own function called `len` in conflict with the built-in `len` function that returns the length of a string or list (*05_01_len.py*)

Listing: 05_01_len.py

```
def len(param):
    print('In our len')

len('abc')
```

When you run this, you will see that it is our new `len` function that is being used, and there is now no way to access the built-in `len` command should we want to use it.

This is our fault for defining a function called `len`. We need to be aware of Python's *keywords* and built-in functions and avoid giving our own functions names like `len`, `print`, `if`, `else`, and etc. But what about the huge number of functions contained in Python modules?

> When it comes to making sure that you don't use names of functions that already exist, these resources are useful:
> - https://www.w3schools.com/python/ — built-in Python keywords.
> - https://www.w3schools.com/python/python_ref_functions.asp – built-in Python functions.

In chapter 4, we saw how we could import the `random` module and then access its functions like this (try it again now in the Shell):

```
>>> import random
>>> random.randint(1, 6)
1
```

Every time we need to use the `randint` function, we have to prefix it with `random` followed by a period. However, if we know we are going to use `randint` a lot in our program, we can `import` just the `randint` function, and then use it without having to specify the module it comes from.

```
>>> from random import randint
>>> randint(1, 6)
1
```

We could also throw caution to the wind and import all the functions in `random` using the `*` (wildcard) like this:

```
>>> from random import *
>>> choice(['apple', 'banana', 'orange'])
'apple'
```

It is safer to be selective and only import the functions that you know you are going to need.

Useful Python Modules

We have used Python's very useful `random` module, and there are many other modules. These modules are often called Python's standard library. There are too many of these to list in full. You will find a complete list here:

`https://docs.python.org/3/library/index.html`

We have met some of these in passing. Some of the most useful, that you might like to take a look at are:

- string - string utilities

- math - math functions (sin, cos etc)

- datetime - manipulating dates and times

- pickle - saving and restoring data structures on file

- json - converting between Python lists and dictionaries and the JSON (JavaScript Object Notation) data format

- tkinter - creating graphical user interfaces

Object-Orientation

Object-orientation has much in common with modules. It shares the same goal of trying to group related things together so that they are easy to maintain and find (called *encapsulation*).

As the name suggests, object-orientation is about objects. We have already been unobtrusively using objects. A 'string' is an object, so when we type:

```
>>> 'abc'.upper()
```

then we are telling the string 'abc' that we want a copy of it, but in uppercase. In object-oriented terms, 'abc' is an *instance* of the built-in *class* str and upper is a *method* on the class str.

Let's look at these new terms in a bit more detail.

A *class* is a similar concept to a *type*. That is, it's a way of expressing what kind of a thing a value is and also what it is capable of doing. For example, the class that represents strings (str) is capable of converting itself into uppercase using the upper() method.

An *instance*, is one example of a particular class, so 'abc' and 'def' are both instances of strings.

A *method* is defined on a class and tells that class how to do something. To use our example again, the string class knows how to make an uppercase version of itself. Methods that are defined on a class are available to all instances of the class.

The term *object* means all instances of any class. In some object-oriented languages, in a somewhat mind-bending way, classes are themselves instances of a *meta-class*.

When you want to call a method, you use a dot before the method name. Hence, converting the string 'abc' to uppercase is done like this 'abc'.upper() and if the string were contained in the variable my_string, then we would call the upper method like this: my_string.upper().

It's not always obvious what class an object is. We can actually find out the class of an object, as shown below (note double underscores before and after the word *class*):

```
>>> 'abc'.__class__
<class 'str'>
>>> [1].__class__
<class 'list'>
>>> 12.34.__class__
<class 'float'>
```

Defining Classes

That's enough of other people's classes, lets make some of our own. We are going to start by making a class that does the job of converting measurements from one unit to another, by multiplying a value by a scale factor.

We will give the class the catchy name `ScaleConverter`. Here we are using what is called *CamelCase* - a mix of uppercase and lower-case letters - to name our class. The convention is that the names of classes all begin with an upper-case letter, to distinguish them from variables that must start with a lower-case letter.

Here is the listing for the whole class, plus a few lines of code to test it. These lines at the end, after the class definition, are just a handy way of testing out code. You could, if you prefer, remove them from the class file and run them in the Shell.

Listing: 05_02_converter_01.py

```
class ScaleConverter:

  def __init__(self, units_from, units_to, factor):
    self.units_from = units_from
    self.units_to = units_to
    self.factor = factor

  def description(self):
    return 'Convert ' + self.units_from + ' to ' + self.units_to

  def convert(self, value):
    return value * self.factor

c1 = ScaleConverter('inches', 'mm', 25)
print(c1.description())
print('converting 2 inches')
print(str(c1.convert(2)) + c1.units_to)
```

This requires some explanation. The first line is fairly obvious, this is saying that we are beginning the definition of a class called `ScaleConverter`. The : on the end shows that all that follows is part of the class definition. The usual indent conventions apply, so everything that follows is part of the class definition until the indent ends.

Inside the `ScaleConverter`, we can see what look like three function definitions. These functions belong to the class, and they cannot be used except via an instance of the class. This kind of function that belongs to a class is called a *method*.

The first method `__init__` looks a bit strange. Not least its name which has two underscore characters on either side of it. When Python is creating a new instance of a class, it automatically calls the method `__init__`. The number of parameters that `__init__` should have depends on how many parameters are supplied when an instance of the class is made. To unravel that, we need to look at this line at the end of the file, which is the start of us using this new class (and not part of the class definition).

```
c1 = ScaleConverter('inches', 'mm', 25)
```

This line creates a new instance of the `ScaleConverter` specifying first the units being converted from and second the units to, as well as the scaling factor.

The `__init__` method must have all these parameters, but must also have a parameter called `self` as the first parameter. The parameter `self` means the newly created instance of the class.

```
def __init__(self, units_from, units_to, factor):
```

Looking at the body of the `__init__` method, we see some assignments.

```
  self.units_from = units_from
  self.units_to = units_to
  self.factor = factor
```

Each of these assignments creates a variable that belongs to the object (`self.units_from` etc) and has its initial value set from the parameters passed in to `__init__` (`units_from` etc).

To recap, when we create a new `ScaleConverter` by typing something like:

```
c1 = ScaleConverter('inches', 'mm', 25)
```

76

Python creates a new instance of ScaleConvertor and assigns the values inches, mm and 25 to its three variables self.units_from, self.units_to and self.factor.

The term *encapsulation* if often used around classes. It is the job of a class to *encapsulate* everything to do with the class. That means both storing data (like the three variables) and things that you might want to do with the data in the form of the description and convert methods.

The first of these methods (description) takes the information that the ScaleConverter knows about (its units) and creates a string that describes it. As with __init__ all methods must have a first parameter of self.

We can now try creating our own instance of ScaleConvertor that converts between the silly units of *apples* and *grapes*, where 74 grapes are equivalent to one apple.

Try it yourself, by running program *05_02_converter_01.py* and then typing the following in the Python Shell:

```
>>> silly_converter = ScaleConverter('apples', 'grapes', 74)
>>> silly_converter.description()
'Convert apples to grapes'
```

The convert method has two parameters – the mandatory self parameter and also a parameter called value. The method simply returns the result of multiplying the value passed in by self.scale.

```
>>> silly_converter.convert(3)
222
```

222 being 3 times 74. So, now we know – 3 apples are equivalent to 74 grapes.

Inheritance

Inheritance is a mechanism that helps to minimize the amount of similar or repeated code in a program. It does this by allowing you to use one class as the basis for another. We will illustrate this by using our ScaleConverter class as the basis for a new class called

`ScaleAndOffsetConverter` that will *inherit* the variables and methods of `ScaleConverter`.

This is now getting firmly into the realm of advnaced Python, so do not worry too much if it seems a little abstract. Many Python programmers get by without ever using inheritance.

The `ScaleConverter` class is okay for units of length and things like that, but it would not work for something like converting temperature from degrees C to degrees F. The formula for this is:

F = C * 1.8 + 32

There is both a scale factor (1.8) and an offset (32).

Let's create a class called `ScaleAndOffsetConverter` that is just like `ScaleConvertor` but as well as having a `factor` also has an `offset`.

One way to do this would simply be to copy the whole of the code for `ScaleConvertor` and change it a bit by adding the extra variable. It might in fact look something like this:

Listing: 05_03_converter_02.py

```
class ScaleAndOffsetConverter:

  def __init__(self, units_from, units_to, factor, offset):
    self.units_from = units_from
    self.units_to = units_to
    self.factor = factor
    self.offset = offset

  def description(self):
    return 'Convert ' + self.units_from + ' to ' + self.units_to

  def convert(self, value):
    return value * self.factor + self.offset

c2 = ScaleAndOffsetConverter('C', 'F', 1.8, 32)
print(c2.description())
print('converting 20C')
print(str(c2.convert(20)) + c2.units_to)
```

Assuming that we need both types of converter in the program we are writing, then this is a bad way of doing it. It is bad because we are repeating code, and one of the unwritten laws of coding is that you should repeat code as rarely as possible. The `description` method is actually identical, and `__init__` is almost the same.

A better way of doing this is to use something called *inheritance*.

The idea of inheritance in classes is that when you want a specialized version of a class that already exists, you inherit all the parent's variables and methods and add new ones or override ones that are different.

Figure 5.1 shows a class diagram for the two classes, showing how `ScaleAndOffsetConverter` inherits from `ScaleConverter` and adds a new variable `offset` and overrides the method `convert` because convert for a `ScaleAndOffsetConverter` will work a bit differently.

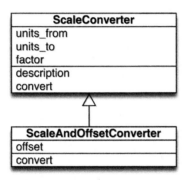

Figure 5.1. Inheritance

Here is the class definition for `ScaleAndOffsetConverter` using inheritance:

```
class ScaleAndOffsetConverter(ScaleConverter):

  def __init__(self, units_from, units_to, factor, offset):
    ScaleConverter.__init__(self, units_from, units_to, factor)
    self.offset = offset

  def convert(self, value):
    return value * self.factor + self.offset
```

The first thing to notice is that, the class definition for `ScaleAndOffsetConverter` has `ScaleConverter` in parentheses after it. That is how you specify the parent class for a class.

The `__init__` method for the new *subclass* of `ScaleConverter` first invokes the `__init__` method of `ScaleConvertor` before defining the new variable `offset`.

The new `convert` method will override the `convert` method in the parent class, as we need to add on the offset for this kind of converter.

You can run and experiment with the two classes together, by running *05_04_converters_final.py.*

```
>>> c1 = ScaleConverter('inches', 'mm', 25)
>>> print(c1.description())
Convert inches to mm
>>> print(str(c1.convert(2)) + c1.units_to)
50mm
>>> c2 = ScaleAndOffsetConverter('C', 'F', 1.8, 32)
>>> print(c2.description())
Convert C to F
>>> print('converting 20C')
converting 20C
>>> print(str(c2.convert(20)) + c2.units_to)
68.0F
```

Making a Module

It is a simple matter to convert these two classes into a module that we can use in other programs.

To turn this file into a module, we should first take the test code off the end of it, and then give the file a more sensible name. Lets call it: *converters.py.* You will find this file in the downloads. The module must be in the same directory as any program that wants to use it.

```
To use the module now, we can just do this:
>>> import converters
>>> c1 = converters.ScaleConverter('inches', 'mm', 25)
>>> print(c1.description())
Convert inches to mm
>>> print('converting 2 inches')
converting 2 inches
>>> print(str(c1.convert(2)) + c1.units_to)
50mm
```

Note that modules do not have to contain a class. A module file can also contain a collection of functions. This is the case for the `random` module, for example.

Exercises

You can find model solutions in the *exercise_solutions* section of the book's downloads and in Appendix B.

It's important to remember that there is no one correct solution to the exercises – if you find a different way of solving the exercise, that works, that's fine.

Exercise 5-1.

Define a class to represent a `person`, that has instance variables on `first_name` and `surname`. Define a method called `full_name` that returns both parts of the name.

Exercise 5-2.

Create a subclasss of Person called Employee that is a subclass of `Person` and adds a new variable `salary` and defines a method called `give_rise` that takes a percentage and increases the salary when called.

Summary

In this chapter we have taken a look at how we can make use of modules and also introduce object-orientation into our programs.

Creating classes may look like a lot of extra effort over simply putting a load of functions into a file and calling it a module. However, you will find that many large complex modules actually make good use of classes. We will meeting classes again in Chapter 7, when we develop a web application.

In the next chapter, we will look at some more advanced features of Python.

6

More Python

This chapter is going to provide you with a bit more practice in writing programs in Python, and also has a grab-bag of useful Python things that don't really fit into earlier chapters. We will need some of these when we begin to look at developing a web application in Chapter 7.

By kind permission of commitstrip.com

More on Lists

We have already found lists to be very useful. Before we look at a new example program that uses lists a lot, we are going to look at a few more things you can do with lists.

List Ranges

Python has a very neat syntax for chopping up lists. The square bracket notation can be used to get a section of a list, rather than a single element of the list. Try the following in the Shell.

```
>>> l = ['a', 'b', 'c', 'd']
>>> l[1:3]
['b', 'c']
```

Bu putting a colon between two numbers inside the square brackets, you can retrieve just a section of the list, starting at the index position of the number to the left of the colon and ending at the second number minus one. Hence, in the example above, we get elements 1 and 2, as Python starts lists at position 0.

You can also use a negative number for the second number, to count back from the end of the list like this:

```
>>> l = ['a', 'b', 'c', 'd']
>>> l[0:-1]
['a', 'b', 'c']
```

The square bracket ranges syntax also works with strings. Try out the following example:

```
>>> text = 'Python is fun'
>>> text[0:-3]
'Python is '
>>>
```

Shuffling

The `random` module has a function called `shuffle` that we will use in the card game example that follows. To use it, you just call the `shuffle` function, passing the list to be shuffled as a parameter. The list elements will be shuffled into a random order.

```
>>> import random
>>> l = ['a', 'b', 'c', 'd']
>>> random.shuffle(l)
>>> l
['c', 'd', 'b', 'a']
>>>
```

Blackjack Example

We'll continue our Python adventure by building up another example. This time, we will make a simplified version of the card game Blackjack. We won't, however, implement betting or some of the more complex aspects of the game.

You will be dealt two cards, where each card has a point value. Aces are worth 1 or 11 at your choice, other cards are worth the value of their *pips* except for Jack, Queen and Kind which are worth 10.

From your start of two cards, you have two options: *twist* (ask for another card) or *stick* (stop playing and finalise your score). If your score goes over 21 then you are said to be *bust* and you get no points.

Being Object-Oriented

To build on what we learned about classes in the last chapter, we are going to use this example to illustrate both building a program in multiple files and making it object-oriented. We will create classes to represent a card and to represent a deck of cards.

Each of these classes will be in their own file and be imported into a main file for the game as a whole.

You can find all the files for this project in the folder *06_card_game* within the *python* folder for the book downloads. The `Card` and `Deck`

6. More Python

classes are defined in the files *card.py* and *deck.py*.

A class for Cards

What should a class for a playing card represent? That is, what should its variables be?

The card class needs to record:

- the suit (clubs, hearts, diamonds and spades)
- the pips (ace, 2 to 10, Jack, Queen and King)

We can then ask what should a card be able to do (it's methods)?

It should be able to:

- calculate its own value (1 to 10) – ignoring aces for now
- display itself in a nice way

Python uses *Unicode* strings. Unicode is what allows Python to use different alphabets and print strange and unusual characters. Unicode actually includes characters to represent the suits of a deck of cards. To access these special characters we need to look up their numbers in a Unicode table. You can easily find such a table with a quick internet search.

Try typing the following into the Shell.

```
>>> '\u2663'
'♣'
```

As you can see we have a special symbol representing the *clubs* suit. We can define variable for each of these suit characters like this inside the Card class like this:

```
class Card:

    clubs = '\u2663'
    spades = '\u2665'
    hearts = '\u2661'
    diamonds = '\u2662'
```

We can then access these from outside the class (say in the Shell) like this:

```
>>> Card.clubs
'♣'
>>>
```

If you want to try this out, then Run *cards.py* in Thonny and then type the command above into the Shell.

While we are at it, let's also create a list of the suits. We don't have an immediate need for it but, thinking forward, when we are creating a deck of 52 cards, it will be useful to be able to loop (also called *iterate*) over the four suits when creating cards to add to the deck. We will call the list `possible_suits`.

```
possible_suits = [clubs, spades, hearts, diamonds]
```

We will treat the pips in a similar way, but just using a letter to represent the card's pips. We can again keep these in an array.

```
pips = ['A', '2', '3', '4', '5', '6', '7', '8', '9', '10',
    'J', 'Q', 'K']
```

The `__init__` method for Card looks like this:

```
def __init__(self, pips, suit):
    self.pips = pips
    self.suit = suit
```

We just transfer the parameters into variables of the same name in the class.

Using what we have so far, if we create a card and print it, we cannot tell much about the card.

```
>>> c = Card('Q', Card.hearts)
>>> print(c)
__main__.Card object at 0x10c8d6b90>
>>>
```

Although this looks almost like an error message. It is actually Python's way of saying that c is an instance of the class `Card`.

It would be nice if, when we printed a card, it would tell us the suit and pips. We can do this by defining a special method in the `Card` class called `__repr__` (representation).

```
def __repr__(self):
    return self.pips + self.suit
```

In this case, the `__repr__` method creates a string from the pips and the suit. Now, when we print a card, we get something much more informative:

```
>>> c = Card('Q', Card.hearts)
>>> print(c)
Q♡
>>>
```

We also need to know the value of any card. We can write a method that does this by dealing with the three cases:

1. An Ace - which we chose to have a value of 11

2. A Jack, Queen or King - 10

3. Any other value of pips will be 2 to 10, so just convert the string to a number using `int` to get the cards value.

```
def value(self):
    if self.pips == 'A': # Ace defaults to 11
        return 11
    elif self.pips in ('J', 'Q', 'K'):
        return 10
    else:
        return int(self.pips)
```

A class for a Deck of Cards

A deck of cards (at least for this game) consists of 52 cards, 13 of each suit. So our `Deck` class should represent all the cards left in the deck (a list).

In addition, the `Deck` should be able to:

- shuffle itself into a random order

- deal a number of cards from the top of the deck into a hand, which we will represent as a list of cards

- as a nice extra, let's make the deck be able to display itself, which will be handy for debugging

Here's the basic structure of the Deck class:

```
from card import Card
from random import shuffle

class Deck:

    def __init__(self):
        self.cards = []
        for suit in Card.possible_suits:
            for pips in Card.possible_pips:
                self.cards.append(Card(pips, suit))
```

As you can see, because `Deck` uses `Card`, we need to import `card` like we would a module. We will also need the `shuffle` function from the `random` module.

You need to ensure that the file with the same name as the module (*card* in this case) is in the same directory as the file importing it - as long as it has *.py* at the end, then it will be found by Python.

The `__init__` method is interesting because it populates a list called `cards` with every possible combination of suit and pips. It does this with one `for` loop nested inside another.

The outer loop iterates over each possible suit and the inner loop over each possible number of pips. A new card is then created and appended to the list of cards.

This idea of *nesting* one `for` loop inside another is quite common, but can be confusing. When you do this, what happens is that for each time around the first (*outer*) loop, the entire innner loop is executed. So, the last line of the listing above (`self.cards.append(Card(pips, suit))`) actually gets run 52 times (4 suits x 13 pips).

As we did with the `Card` class, we can define an `__repr__` method to print out the deck nicely.

```
def __repr__(self):
    return '<Deck: ' + str(self.cards) + '>'
```

This method mostly relies on the ability of `Card` to print itself nicely, converting the list of cards to a string and putting some marks around the string so that we can see it's an instance of `Deck`.

We can test the `Deck` class out by running *deck.py* and then typing the following in the Shell.

```
>>> d = Deck()
>>> d
<Deck: [A♣, 2♣, 3♣, 4♣, 5♣, 6♣, 7♣, 8♣, 9♣, 10♣, J♣, Q♣, K♣,
A♠, 2♠, 3♠, 4♠, 5♠, 6♠, 7♠, 8♠, 9♠, 10♠, J♠, Q♠, K♠,
A♡, 2♡, 3♡, 4♡, 5♡, 6♡, 7♡, 8♡, 9♡, 10♡, J♡, Q♡, K♡,
A◇, 2◇, 3◇, 4◇, 5◇, 6◇, 7◇, 8◇, 9◇, 10◇, J◇, Q◇, K◇]>
>>>
```

Clearly playing a game with that deck of cards would be a bit predictable as the cards are all in order. Let's add a `shuffle` method to the class.

```
def shuffle(self):
    shuffle(self.cards)
```

All this method does is use the `shuffle` method from `random` to shuffle the `cards` list in the deck.

Finally, let's create a `deal` method. This will have two parameters, the number of cards to deal and the list to put the cards into.

```
def deal(self, n, hand):
    for i in range(0, n):
        hand.append(self.cards.pop())
```

The `deal` method uses a `for` loop to repeat the action of popping a card off the deck and appending it to the list supplied. Here the `hand` variable will be an existing list of cards to be modified by this method.

We can try all this out in the console:

```
>>> d = Deck()
>>> d
<Deck: [A♣, 2♣, 3♣, 4♣, 5♣, 6♣, 7♣, 8♣, 9♣, 10♣, J♣, Q♣, K♣,
A♠, 2♠, 3♠, 4♠, 5♠, 6♠, 7♠, 8♠, 9♠, 10♠, J♠, Q♠, K♠,
A♡, 2♡, 3♡, 4♡, 5♡, 6♡, 7♡, 8♡, 9♡, 10♡, J♡, Q♡, K♡,
A◇, 2◇, 3◇, 4◇, 5◇, 6◇, 7◇, 8◇, 9◇, 10◇, J◇, Q◇, K◇]>
>>> d.shuffle()
```

```
>>> d
<Deck: [5♡, 7♠, 8♣, A♠, 6◇, 7◇, 3♠, J♣, 8♠, J♠, 2♠, K♡, 9♣,
A◇, Q◇, 10◇, J♡, 9◇, 7♡, 3◇, 9♠, 2♣, 10♠, 10♣, Q♣,
4◇, 5◇, Q♡, 6♠, K♠, 10♡, 5♣, J◇, 6♡, 3♣, 8♡, 7♣, K♣,
9♡, A♡, K◇, 4♠, 3♡, 4♡, 4♣, Q♠, 6♣, 5♠, A♣, 8◇, 2◇, 2♡]>
>>> hand = []
>>> d.deal(7, hand)
>>> hand
[2♡, 2◇, 8◇, A♣, 5♠, 6♣, Q♠]
>>> d
<Deck: [5♡, 7♠, 8♣, A♠, 6◇, 7◇, 3♠, J♣, 8♠, J♠, 2♠, K♡, 9♣,
A◇, Q◇, 10◇, J♡, 9◇, 7♡, 3◇, 9♠, 2♣, 10♠, 10♣, Q♣,
4◇, 5◇, Q♡, 6♠, K♠, 10♡, 5♣, J◇, 6♡, 3♣, 8♡, 7♣, K♣,
9♡, A♡, K◇, 4♠, 3♡, 4♡, 4♣]>
>>>
```

As you can see, the cards are actually coming off the end of the deck. But that's fine. The important thing is that the cards have been removed from the deck and added to the hand.

Blackjack

By making classes for Card and Deck, we have made a number of things possible:

- The code for the game itself should be very much easier

- We have code that could potentially be used to code other card games

- Our main program file should be shorter and easier to maintain, as we now have separate files for the Card and Deck classes, that we can mostly ignore, unless we uncover a bug in them.

Turning our attention to the Blackjack game itself, we will build it up one step at a time. I would always recommend this approach. Get the simplest thing working, test it, then add another feature, and test again. If you try and write all the code in one go and then test, it makes debugging very much harder.

You can find the final code in *blackjack_final.py*. You will also find intermediate files here called *blackjack_1.py, blackjack_2.py* etc. that you can use to follow along with the development of the game.

Many programmers would create another class here called Blackjack.

You could imagine a scenario where you might have a generic class called `CardGame` that had a deck, knew whose turn it was, could do various things that happen in any card game and could be specialised by a subclass for a particular game such as Blackjack. Other developers, like me, would argue that the time you do that is when you come to write your second card game. But, in this case, we won't create a class for Blackjack.

Now, let's start work on a function that we will call `play_game`. This function's job is to let the user play a single game of Blackjack until they either stick or go bust.

Listing: python/card_game/blackjack_1.py

```python
from card import *
from deck import *

def play_game():
    deck = Deck()
    deck.shuffle()
    hand = []
    deck.deal(2, hand)
    while True:
        print(hand)
        action = input('t-twist or s-stick: ')
        if action == 't':
            deck.deal(1, hand)
        elif action == 's':
            print('Sticking')
            break

play_game()
```

We start by importing the things we are going to need, i.e. everything from both `card` and `deck`. This will actually just import the `Card` and `Deck` classes.

The function `play_game` creates a new deck, shuffles it and then deals two cards into a list called `hand`.

We now have a loop that:

1. displays the player's hand

2. prompts the user to twist or stick

3. repeats steps 1 and 2 until the player chooses *stick*

The player can choose to enter *t* to twist (take another card) or enter *s* to stick. If they enter *t*, another card is dealt from the deck to the hand; if they decide to stick, the break command jumps out of the while loop and the game ends.

We already have a fairly rudimentary game, and we could use it – but we would have to work out the scores ourselves, and put up with the fact that it doesn't detect when our hand is bust.

Scoring a hand is made tricky by the fact that an Ace can either count as 1 or 11. We will simplify this by saying that an ace is worth 11, unless that hand busts, in which case it's worth 1.

We could decide if a card is an ace by using the condition card.pips == 'A'. However, to make the code even more readable (and illustrate a point) we will instead add a new method called is_ace to the Card class like this:

```
def is_ace(self):
    return (self.pips == 'A')
```

Back in the main blackjact file now, here is the function score_hand.

```
def score_hand(cards):
    score = 0
    have_ace = False
    for card in cards:
        if card.is_ace():
            have_ace = True
        score += card.value()
        if score > 21 and have_ace:
            score -= 10 # lower ace value
            have_ace = False # only do this once
    return score
```

We can test this out in isolation by creating a hand (a list of cards) and calling score_hand like this:

```
>>> score_hand([Card('7', Card.clubs), Card('A', Card.clubs)])
18
>>> score_hand([Card('7', Card.clubs), Card('A', Card.clubs),
    Card('Q', Card.hearts)])
18
>>> score_hand([Card('7', Card.clubs), Card('A', Card.clubs),
    Card('8', Card.hearts)])
16
```

To help the player decide whether to twist or stick, we can display the score for the hand after the contents of the hand. To do this we will use a new function called `display_hand` that will replace the simple `print` command that we have been using so far.

```
def display_hand(hand):
    score = score_hand(hand)
    print('Your hand: ' + str(hand) + ' (' + str(score) + ')')
```

These two new functions are integrated into the game in the program *blackjack_2.py*. Now, when we play the game, we can see the value of our hand.

```
Your hand: [9◇, J♣] (19)
t-twist or s-strick: t
Your hand: [9◇, J♣, K♣] (29)
t-twist or s-strick: t
Your hand: [9◇, J♣, K♣, Q♡] (39)
t-twist or s-strick: s
Sticking
```

However, there is nothing to stop us twisting long after we have gone bust. So, let's add in some code to detect going bust and end the game. Here is the revised `play_game` function. I have also put `play_game` into a `while` loop so that a new game starts as soon as the previous one ends. You can find this in *blackjack_final.py*.

```
def play_game():
    deck = Deck()
    deck.shuffle()
    hand = []
    deck.deal(2, hand)
    print('\n\nNew Game')
```

```
    while True:
        score = score_hand(hand)
        display_hand(hand)
        action = input('t-twist or s-strick: ')
        if action == 't':
            deck.deal(1, hand)
            score = score_hand(hand)
            if score > 21:
                display_hand(hand)
                print('BUST!')
                break
        elif action == 's':
            print('Sticking with :' + str(score))
            break

while True:
    play_game()
```

The going-bust detection happens after a twist – after displaying the final hand, it breaks from the while loop to start a new game.

Exercises 6-1 to 6-3 are all based on this example. Try them now if you want, or wait until the end of the chapter.

Exceptions

At various points in your Python adventure, you have probably come across error messages. Open the deliberately buggy program *06_01_errors_1.py* and run it.

Listing: 06_01_errors_1.py

```
x = input('Enter a number: ')
y = x * x
print(y)
```

When you run it, enter the value 12 when prompted. You should see an error like this.

```
Enter a number: 12
Traceback (most recent call last):
  File "06_01_errors_1.py", line 2, in <module>
    y = x * x
TypeError: can't multiply sequence by non-int of type 'str'
>>>
```

This kind of error message is very useful, because it tells us what the problem is (although this can be a bit cryptic) and also where the error occurred (line 2).

After the programs *crashes* with an error like this, we can do further investigation using the Shell. There is obviously something wrong with x, so if we just type x in the Shell, we can see what value it has, like this.

```
>>> x
'12'
```

And there's the problem – x is a string not a number (it has quote marks around it). We have a bug in the code: the error message is telling us our code is wrong, because even though we entered 12 in response to the `input` command, that 12 is a string and so Python does not know how to multiply strings together. We can fix the error by converting x into an int like this (06_02_errors_2.py).

Listing: 06_02_errors_2.py

```
x = int(input('Enter a number: '))
y = x * x
print(y)
```

Run it again and again enter 12 when prompted.

```
>>> %Run 06_02_errors_2.py
Enter a number: 12
144
>>>
```

Now we are getting the result we expect – 144. We have fixed one bug, but the code is still unsafe. Run the program again, and this time enter *abc*.

```
>>> %Run 06_02_errors_2.py
Enter a number: abc
Traceback (most recent call last):
  File "/Users/si/Dropbox/Books in progress/50
      Coding/code/coding_book/python/06_01_errors_2.py", line
      1, in <module>
    x = int(input('Enter a number: '))
ValueError: invalid literal for int() with base 10: 'abc'
>>>
```

Quite reasonably, the Python int function is unable to interpret *abc* as a number and is said to have *thrown* an error.

This is different from our first error, because, in this case, we have no control over what a user might type in. We can however catch the error that is thrown and handle it in our own way, as demonstrated in 06_03_errors_3.py.

Listing: 06_03_errors_3.py

```
x_str = input('Enter a number: ')
try:
    x = int(x_str)
    y = x * x
    print(y)
except:
    print('You must enter a number')
```

Try running it a few times, entering numbers or text. As you can see we have now made our program much more robust.

JSON

Complex software systems often need to move data about between different programs. Not all programs are written in Python. To move data structures from one program to another they are usually *serialized* into text. For a while the preferred format for this was XML (Extensible Markup Language). But this has pretty much universally replaced by JSON (JavaScript Object Notation).

JSON looks very much like Python lists and dictionaries in its syntax, and a Python data structure can easily be serialized into a string, or a string containing text in a JSON format converted into a Python data structure.

Listing *06_04_json_dumps.py* shows how the movies example, from Chapter 3, of a list of dictionaries can be converted into a string in JSON format.

Listing: 06_04_json_dumps.py

```python
import json

movies = [
    {
        'title':'Jaws',
        'director':'Steven Spielberg',
        'duration': 124
    },
    {
        'title':'The Godfather',
        'director':'Francis Ford Coppola,',
        'duration': 175
    },
    {
        'title':'Baby Driver',
        'director':'Edgar Wright',
        'duration': 115
    },
]

text = json.dumps(movies)
```

First we have to import the json module. Its dumps (short for *dump string*) function converts any Python data structure (strings, numbers, lists, dictionaries etc.) into a string.

When we list the string, by typing text in the console, it looks disturbingly similar to the original Python. We can check that it definitely is a string by asking Python to see what class it is, using the __class__ method (double underscores each side of class).

```
>>> text
'[{"title": "Jaws", "director": "Steven Spielberg",
    "duration": 124}, {"title": "The Godfather", "director":
    "Francis Ford Coppola,", "duration": 175}, {"title":
    "Baby Driver", "director": "Edgar Wright", "duration":
    115}]'
>>> text.__class__
<class 'str'>
```

As you can see, the class is str (string).

Going the other way and converting a JSON string into Python objects is accomplished using the json.loads (short for emphload string) function. This is illustrated in *06_05_json_loads.py*.

Listing: 06_05_json_loads.py

```
import json

s = '{"title": "Jaws", "director": "Steven Spielberg",
    "duration": 124}'

dict = json.loads(s)

print(dict['title'])
```

The ability to use either single quotes or double quotes to denote strings comes in handy here, as we can put the whole string in single quotes and use double quotes around the keys and values in the dictionary or vice-versa.

Exercises

Try out these exercises to test your knowledge. If you get stuck, you can see model solutions for these in the *exercise_solutions* directory of the book downloads and in Appendix B.

Exercise 6-1.

Add some code to *blackjack_final.py* so that, if the player sticks, then the next 5 cards that would be drawn are displayed.

Exercise 6-2.

Modify *blackjack_final.py* so that, rather than start a new deck of cards for each hand, the same deck is used until all the cards have gone.

Exercise 6-3

Modify *blackjack_final.py* so that printing occurs in a ticker-type way, where there is a short delay between each letter of the text being printed. Hint: search for python print without new line and Python `time.sleep`.

Exercise 6-4

Modify the tic-tac-toe game from Chapter 4, (*04_10_xo_5.py*) so that it does not crash if someone enters a move position that is not a number.

Summary

In this chapter we have worked through another game example and also learnt about exceptions and the JSON data format. You should now be starting to get comfortable with Python and might like to try writing a few simple programs yourself.

In the next chapter, we will look at database programming.

7

Databases

In this chapter we will take a look at relational databases and the language SQL (Structured Query Language) used to create tables, add data and query the database. We will use the light-weight SQLite database as an easy-to-use system to experiment with.

Database programmers and database administrators (DBAs) are always in demand in the software industry, as the database (where all the data is) is arguably the most important part of any software system.

What we learn here about databases will also help us in the next chapter where we look at how web applications are made.

Relational Databases

Despite having been around for half a century, relational databases are still the dominant database technology used in computer systems. The relational part of relational databases refers to the relationships from one table to another. Tables of data look familiar to a spreadsheet user. Each row is a record of data, with the columns being different attributes of the table. For example, a table to represent movie titles might look like Table 7.1.

The id or *identifier* column provides a unique way of identifying a particular row or *record* in the table. This is called a *primary key*.

id	title	director	duration
1	Jaws	Steven Spielberg.	124
2	The Godfather	Francis Ford Coppola	174
3	Baby Driver	Edgar Wright	115
4	E.T.	Steven Spielberg	105

Table 7.1.: A Relational database table to represent movie titles.

We could use the *title* as a primary key, but strings don't generally make good primary keys because they can use letters in different cases, or other slight changes. For example *Godfather* instead of *The Godfather* or *ET* instead of *E.T.*. So it has become a standard part of using a relational database to allocate an *id* when a row is created. Once allocated, this *id* can never be changed, and the *id* will always be unique – by the simple expedient of allocating numbers in order, with no repetition.

Generally movie directors direct more than one movie in their careers. This is referred to as a one-to-many relationship. So, if we were trying to find all the films directed by Steven Spielberg, then we would need to be sure that we spelled it the exact same way in each row of the movie titles table. Once again a string does not make a reliable key. Also, with just one movie titles table, there is nowhere to store information about the director – perhaps his date of birth and country of origin. The answer is to have two tables, one for movie titles and one for directors, as shown in Tables 7.2 and 7.3.

id	title	director_id	duration
1	Jaws	1	124
2	The Godfather	2	174
3	Baby Driver	3	115
4	E.T.	1	105

Table 7.2.: A Relational database table to represent just movie titles

id	name	date_of_birth	nationality
1	Steven Spielberg	1946-12-18	USA
2	Francis Ford Coppola	1939-04-07	USA
3	Edgar Wright	1974-04-18	UK

Table 7.3.: A Relational database table to represent movie directors.

Now Table 7.2 no longer stores the director's name, but stores the id of a row for the director in Table 7.3. This pulling-out of data that should belong in its own table is called *normalization*. Although there are formal definitions for exactly how normalized a set of database tables are, you can just use common sense most of the time. For instance, you may now be thinking about whether nationality should actually be a link to yet another table, where information about countries is stored.

If you start thinking that maybe something should be a separate table, then the answer is usually *yes it should*.

Note that I have deliberately chosen the SQL format for dates, where the year is specified first followed by the month number and day of the month, separated by dashes. That's because it has the useful property, that when sorted alphabetically, the dates are in correct order.

SQLite

To learn about databases we will use a light-weight relational database called SQLite that is perfect for our purpose of learning about relational databases and the query language that they use called SQL (pronounced as both the three letters spelled out and as *sequel* – take your pick).

In Chapter 8 we will be using the django web framework. Installing django also installs SQLite on your computer, so you may as well install django now.

The Command Line

To install django (and hence SQLite) we are going to go full-hacker and use a terminal or command line to run commands.

The *terminal* is often depicted as the quintessential hacker experience in movies – the hero or heroine furiously tapping a way at a keyboard, *talking* to the computer in order to save the world.

Windows, MacOS and Linux all include a terminal application, which is a simple window into which one can type operating system com-

By kind permission of commitstrip.com

mands. This is rather like Thonny's Python Shell area, except that the commands can be operating system commands to install software, run programs or communicate with other computers.

On Windows, there is a terminal application called *Powershell* that you can find in the *Start menu*. When it comes to MacOS, the Terminal application can be found in the *Utilities* section of *Applications* and Linux users can find a Terminal in various places depending on the flavour of Linux that they use.

In this chapter and chapter 8, we will use the command line both for installing Python-related software, and running Python programs. So, if you have been using Thonny's built-in Python, you now need to take the step of installing stand-alone Python on your computer.

If you are a Linux user, then there is nothing to do – a recent version of Python 3 and pip (Package Installer for Python) should already be installed.

To install Python 3 (the version we are using in this book) for your platform, you should follow to the instructions here:

```
https://www.python.org/downloads/
```

This will download an installer that will install both the Python language itself and pip.

If you are installing on Windows, make sure that you select the option to *Add Python exe to path* (highlighted in Figure **??**).

Figure 7.2. The Windows installer for Python.

Once installed, if you are using Windows, open the PowerShell and run the command `python` (Figure 7.3). For Mac and Linux, do the same in a Terminal. If all is well, you should get a report that you are using Python 3. You can try out a few Python commands here if you like.

If typing `python` into a Mac OS Terminal results in an error message, then you may have to use `python3` (with a 3 on the end) to run Python.

Instaling django

As I mentioned, earlier in this chapter, we will be using django extensively in Chapter 8 and the django installer also installs SQLite. So rather than install SQLite on its own we might as well install django now, even through we won't need it until Chapter 8.

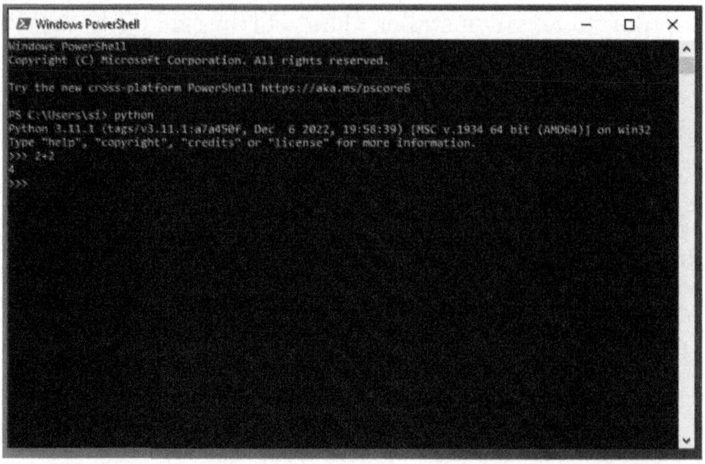

Figure 7.3. The Python Shell in Windows PowerShell.

> *pip* (Package Installer for Python) is a command line tool for installing, uninstalling and updating Python-based software. This can be just modules that aren't included in the standard Python install, or they can be entire Python-based systems such as django.

We will use the *pip* package installer to install django. This requires us to enter the command:

```
> pip install django
```

This can be in the Windows Power Shell, or in a Linux or Mac OS Terminal. It does not matter which directory you are in when you run the command. Note that, depending on your Python environment, on a Mac or Linux machine you may have to use the command *pip3* rather than *pip*.

Now that django is installed, SQLite and its command line tool will also be installed. You can check this by running the command `sqlite3` as shown below. Note that to exit SQLite use the command `.quit`.

```
$ sqlite3
SQLite version 3.37.0 2021-12-09 01:34:53
Enter ".help" for usage hints.
```

```
Connected to a transient in-memory database.
Use ".open FILENAME" to reopen on a persistent database.
```

Here, all we have done is issue the command `sqlite3` to start an SQLite shell.

If you are using Windows, SQLite will be installed, but frustratingly, the command line utility will not be accessible from the Powershell. The easiest way to get access to an sqllite command line is to go to: https://sqlite.org/download.html and, in the section *Precompiled Binaries for Windows* download the ZIP file *sqlite-tools-win32-x86*. Extract the downloaded ZIP archive and, within it, you will find a program called *sqlite3.exe*. When you run this program a SQLite shell like the one shown in Figure 7.4 will open.

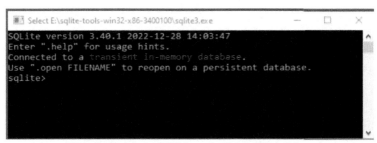

Figure 7.4. A SQLite shell in Windows.

Creating a Database

Whatever operating system you are using, you will see that, in its opening message, SQLite is very sensibly suggesting that we might want to open (or in our case create) a new database using the .open command. Call your database *test_db* and open it like this.

```
sqlite> .open test_db.sqlite3
```

This will create a file called *test_db.sqlite3* that will contain all the tables of data that we are about to create. If a database with that filename already exists then the existing database will be opened rather than a new one be created.

107

Creating Tables

The SQLite command line allows us to issue two different types of command to the database. Commands like .open are specific to SQLite, whereas anything else we type into the command line is assumed to be in SQL. Remember SQLite is the database software and SQL is the language we use to manipulate the database and query it. SQL is what we will use to create tables, populate them with data and modify them. We can then query the database to produce tabular reports of data that we are interested in. We can create the equivalent of Table 8-2 using the command:

```
sqlite> create table movie_titles (id INTEGER PRIMARY KEY,
    title STRING, director_id INTEGER, duration INTEGER);
```

Once you have entered the SQLite command line tool, it works in much the same way as the Python Shell. You enter commands, and is responds with messages. Instead of Python's >>> prompting you to enter a command, SQLite prompts you with sqlite>.

If your commands are long, you can use multiple lines by simply pressing the ENTER key between any words of the command. The command will only run when you end a line with a semicolon (;). Here is an example of a command split over two lines, that you will meet again shortly. In this case the ENTER key was pressed after the word directors. SQLite puts the prompt ...> at the start of the continuation line.

```
sqlite> select * from movie_titles, directors
    ...> where directors.id = movie_titles.director_id;
```

The format of the create table command is firstly to specify the table name (movie_titles) and then the fields that the table should have in parentheses separated by commas. The first of these is id, which is specified as being an INTEGER and also a PRIMARY KEY. This will ensure that every time we create a new row in the table, that row will automatically be allocated a new and unique (for this table) value of id. The title is specified as being a STRING and then we have an INTEGER field for director_id in anticipation of having a second table of directors to link to using the id. This type of field that references a key on another table is called a *foreign key*.

Note that every SQL command must end in a semicolon ;. You will at first often find that nothing happens when you hit the Enter key other than the command prompt moves onto a second line. If this happens, you can just type a semicolon and then hit Enter. It's also worth noting that SQL is not case-sensitive. It does not matter if you use upper or lower case commands.

While we are at it, let's make a the table for the directors.

```
sqlite> create table directors (id INTEGER PRIMARY KEY,
   ...> name STRING, date_of_birth DATE, nationality STRING);
```

Inserting Data

We can start by adding a row to the movie_titles table for our first film, Jaws. To do this, we use the insert SQL command like this:

```
sqlite> insert into movie_titles (title, duration)
   ...> values ('Jaws', 124);
```

The insert command is really the insert into command, and starts with the name of the table that we want to create a new row in. When creating a new row, we need to specify the fields, that we want to add data for, in parentheses. Then we have the word values followed by another set of parentheses with the values for the fields that we specified. So, in this case, we want to set the title to 'Jaws' and the duration to 124. Note that, for now, we are not specifying the director_id – we will come and add that later, after we have added some data to the directors table.

Configuring SQLite output

We can check what's in the movie_titles table using the SQL command select, like this:

```
sqlite> select * from movie_titles;
1|Jaws||124
```

The * after select means *all fields*. The output doesn't tell us which field each value is, but we can change the formatting into something easier to read by issuing the following two special SQLite commands:

```
sqlite> .headers on
sqlite> .mode column
sqlite> select * from movie_titles;
id  title  director_id  duration
1   Jaws                124
```

That's much easier to read.

Inserting the Remaining Data

We can now add some more rows to the movies table using the insert commands, before checking what we have in the table using a select query:

```
sqlite> insert into movie_titles (title, duration) values ('The Godfather', 174);
sqlite> insert into movie_titles (title, duration) values ('Baby Driver', 115);
sqlite> insert into movie_titles (title, duration) values ('E.T.', 105);
sqlite> select * from movie_titles;
id  title        director_id duration
1   Jaws                     124
2   The Godfather            174
3   Baby Driver              115
4   E.T.                     105
sqlite>
```

Now populate the directors table, and then query it to check the contents.

```
sqlite> insert into directors (name, date_of_birth, nationality)
   ...> values ('Steven Spielberg', '1946-12-18', 'USA');
sqlite> insert into directors (name, date_of_birth, nationality)
   ...> values ('Francis Ford Coppola', '1939-04-07', 'USA');
sqlite> insert into directors (name, date_of_birth, nationality)
   ...> values ('Edgar Wright', '1974-04-18', 'UK');
sqlite> select * from directors;
id  name                 date_of_birth nationality
1   Steven Spielberg     1946-12-18    USA
2   Francis Ford Coppola 1939-04-07    USA
3   Edgar Wright         1974-04-18    UK
sqlite>
```

Linking the Tables

We now have our two tables but need to link them together so that each `movie_title` row has a `director_id`. SQL has quite a natural language style to it. To set the `director_id` to 1 (Steven Spielberg) for rows of the `movie_titles` table with ids 1 and 4 (Jaws and E.T.) we can just do:

```
sqlite> update movie_titles set director_id=1
   ...> where id=1 or id=4;
sqlite> select * from movie_titles;
id  title           director_id duration
-------------------------------------------
1   Jaws            1           124
2   The Godfather               174
3   Baby Driver                 115
4   E.T.            1           105
sqlite>
```

That just leaves us with `director_ids` for *The Godfather* and *Baby Driver* to be added like this:

```
sqlite> update movie_titles set director_id=2 where id=2;
sqlite> update movie_titles set director_id=3 where id=3;
sqlite> select * from movie_titles;
id  title           director_id duration
-------------------------------------------
1   Jaws            1           124
2   The Godfather 2             174
3   Baby Driver   3             115
4   E.T.            1           105
sqlite>
```

Modifying Rows

You can use the `update` command to modify a row or rows of the table. So, for example, if you wanted to change the title E.T. to `Extra Terrestrial` in the `movie_titles` table, you could do so like this:

```
sqlite> update movie_titles
```

```
    ...> set title='Extra Terrestrial'
    ...> where id=4;
sqlite> select * from movie_titles;
id  title               director_id duration
--  ------------------- ----------- --------
1   Jaws                1           124
2   The Godfather       2           174
3   Baby Driver         3           115
4   Extra Terrestrial 1             105
sqlite>
```

When using `update` like this, be careful, because if you do not include a `while`, to narrow the rows the `update` should apply to, all of the rows will have their title changed to `'Extra Terrestrial'`.

Querying

Now that we have a database with some data in it, we can try using queries to extract data from it. Currently, when we do a simple select on the `movie_titles` table, we don't see the directors name. To do this we have to do a query that *joins* the `movie_titles` and `directors` tables, like this:

```
sqlite> select * from movie_titles, directors
    ...> where directors.id = movie_titles.director_id;
id  title       director_id duration id name                  date_of_birth nationality
--- ----------- ----------- -------- -- --------------------- ------------- -----------
1   Jaws        1           124      1  Steven Spielberg      1946-12-18    USA
2   The Godfather 2         174      2  Francis Ford Coppola  1939-04-07    USA
3   Baby Driver 3           115      3  Edgar Wright          1974-04-18    UK
4   E.T.        1           105      1  Steven Spielberg      1946-12-18    USA
sqlite>
```

In this query, the `select` references both tables and has a second line with a `where` clause that matches the `id` of the directors table (`directors.id`) with the `director_id` field of the `movie_titles` table (`movie_titles.director_id`). By using a `*`, all the fields of both tables are included, which we don't really need. We can specify which fields we want like this:

```
sqlite> select movie_titles.title, directors.name,
    movie_titles.duration
    ...> from movie_titles, directors
    ...> where directors.id = movie_titles.director_id;
title          name                     duration
```

```
----------------------------------------------
Jaws           Steven Spielberg    124
The Godfather Francis Ford Coppola 174
Baby Driver    Edgar Wright        115
E.T.           Steven Spielberg    105
sqlite>
```

If we wanted to find out all films with a duration of over 120 minutes, we could do:

```
sqlite> select title, duration from movie_titles
   ...> where duration > 120;
title          duration
----------------------
Jaws           124
The Godfather 174
sqlite>
```

Here, we have not prefixed the fields we want to be displayed with the name of the table, because there is only one table used in the query, so they can't be ambiguous.

The SQL count command can be used to find the number of rows, rather than reporting the actual row detail. For example to count the number movies, in the movie_titles table, you can do:

```
sqlite> select count(*) from movie_titles;
count(*)
--
4
sqlite>
```

SQL Injection

A security flaw that used to be popular to exploit is called SQL injection. This relied on the fact that some systems took what the user typed into a search field and used it as part of an SQL query. Since you could put anything in this search string, hackers would put SQL commands to grant themselves access to the machine and take it over.

Great care has to be taken by the developer with such features, as SQL has powerful commands that can empty or delete a table with just a few words.

SQL from Python

We have used django's models to interact with the database. However, as an alternative, you can interact with a database directly from Python without installing django. In fact the `sqlite3` Python package, that allows you to do this, is part of the standard distribution of Python. To try this out, you need to open a Terminal or Power Shell and change directory to the same directory as our test database file (*test_db.sqlite3*).

Then enter the following commands in the Python console.

```
>>> import sqlite3
>>> connection = sqlite3.connect('test_db.sqlite3')
>>> cursor = connection.cursor()
>>> cursor.execute('select * from movie_titles;')
<sqlite3.Cursor object at 0x100d8fb90>
>>> cursor.fetchone()
(1, 'Jaws', 1, 124)
>>> cursor.fetchall()
[(2, 'The Godfather', 2, 174), (3, 'Baby Driver', 3, 115),
    (4, 'E.T.', 1, 105)]
```

After importing the `sqlite3` package a `connection` is created to the database file that we want to use. The package uses the concept of a *cursor* to cope with situations where the database might have very large numbers or records, that might make Python slow or run out of memory (if it tried to load them all at the same time). The cursor can be asked just to fetch the next record (`fetchone`) or all the remaining records (`fetchall`) or a specified number of records (`fetchsome(number)`).

The strange looking text `0x100d8fb90` is a unique token (name) that uniquely identifies the cursor being used. There is no particular reason for the Python sqlite3 package to tell us this number, but it does so anyway.

NoSQL Databases

NoSQL (Not Only SQL) databases is a general term encompassing a whole range of different database management systems that are not table centred. The most popular of these systems, like mongoDB, are document-based and allow the efficient storage of large documents, usually in JSON format.

Exercises

As well as exploring SQL and trying out queries, the following exercises will give you some practice at using SQL. You can also find the whole test database file from the book downloads – it's in the folder called *sql* and is called *test_db.sqlite3*. So you can open that database from the SQLite command line if your database gets in a mess.

Model solutions to the exercises can also be found in the *exercise_solutions* folder and in Appendix B.

Exercise 7-1

Extend the following query, so that is also displays the name of the film's director.

```
select title, duration from movie_titles where duration >
    120;
```

Exercise 7-2.

Write a Python program using the sqlite3 module to print each director and the number of movies credited to them in the test database.

Summary

In this chapter you have got to grips with a bit of database design and programming. We have only touched on SQL, so you may find

yourself wanting to find out more. There are many good books available on databases, and most online SQL tutorials will reinforce what
you have learnt here.

In Chapter 8, we are going to turn our attention away from games
and look at how we can use the django python web framework to
code an altogether more real-world application that takes us all the
way from database to web browser.

8

Web Applications

Everything we have done so far might be termed *pure* Python programming. This is a necessary skill and will serve you well, but the practical reality is that small individual stand-alone Python programs are not what most software systems are about. Yes, small programs have a place as scripts to carry out some useful function, but software systems of any size are a lot more complex.

In this chapter we take a look at the more realistic scenario of web applications. We will use the SQLite database and the django web framework to build up a Python-based web application.

The example is that of a contacts list, and serves to demonstrate a web application from database to browser. Although the application is primarily Python, you will also meet some HTML, JavaScript and SQL on the way.

Websites

When you visit a website in your browser, there is quite a lot going on behind the scenes. Let's start by looking at how a website works. The numbers in the description correspond to the numbered arrows in 8.2.

1. First, the web browser requests a specific page from the web server using the IP (internet protocol).

By kind permission of commitstrip.com

2. The web server sends a web page back to the browser for it to display. This web page contains information about what to display, but also program code in JavaScript. This JavaScript allows the web page to act like a program running in the browser.

3. The next step might be that the web page needs to fetch some data to display (perhaps a list of contacts). This data is returned by the web server's API (Application Programmer Interface), usually in JSON format.

4. The website can now use this received data to change what's displayed in the browser.

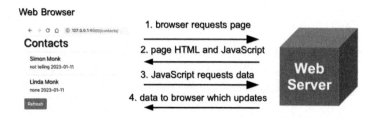

Figure 8.2. A web browser and web server.

Implementing a Website

Most software developed today is for web servers. These systems are made from various lumps of ready-made software, such as database management systems, infrastructure, middleware and web frameworks. 8.3 summarises the architectural layers involved in the example project for this chapter.

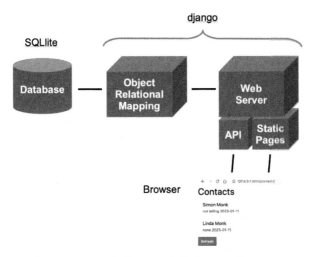

Figure 8.3. A Layered Software System

> In our small example programs, so far, data has just been kept in Python lists or dictionaries assigned to variables. In the real world, this is not good enough, because there might be millions of data records and thousands of people accessing the data at the same time. What's more, if the program exits, all that data disappears.
>
> Databases (or more correctly Database Management Systems) address all these limitations, storing large amounts of data in a way that lots of users can access simultaneously and that is stored in a persistent and reliable manner.

In this example, an SQLite database is used to hold the data used by the system as tables. This type of database is called a *relational* database, and, as the name suggests, SQLite is a light-weight database, not really intended for dealing with large sets of data or lots of users.

The *django* framework provides a way of accessing that data in convenient Python form in what is called an Object Relational Mapping (ORM) – *object*, because the relational table of the database is represented as a Python class. Django allows you to use different database management systems. So, for real world applications, you would probably pick something like Prostgress rather than SQLite, as SQLite is only designed for a small number of simultaneous users and fairly small quantities of data.

In this example django also acts as a web server but, as with the choice of database management system, in a real application a more powerful web server like *nginx* would most likely be used, to do the heavy lifting for large numbers of users, working with django to do the clever bit of providing the API.

Visual Studio Code

Thonny is great for learning Python, but as soon as you start to develop a more realistic example project, its limitations become apparent. Thonny is not designed to deal with complex directory structures of source code. So it's time to take the training wheels off and introduce a different code editor or IDE (Integrated Development Environment). *Visual Studio Code* (lets call it *VS Code*), is very popular amongst programmers. It manages to hit the sweet-spot between a really simple text editor and a full-featured IDE. Even though VS Code is a Microsoft product, it is free to download and use and is certainly not restricted to use with Microsoft frameworks – which is just as well, as we are using Python (which has nothing to do with Microsoft). VS Code is also available for Windows, Mac and Linux.

To install VS Code, visit the URL below and select the download for your operating system.

```
https://code.visualstudio.com/download
```

Let's try out VS Code by opening the code for this chapter's example project. So, start VS Code and then select *Open Folder..* from the *File* menu. Then navigate to the folder where the books code downloads are contained and, within that, open the folder called *django/contacts_project* with VS Code. You should see something

By kind permission of commitstrip.com

like Figure 8.5.

Figure 8.5. The code for the example project for this chapter in VS Code.

The navigation area on the left allows you easily to access the different files in the folder and subfolders. Try clicking on some of the files to see the code.

Once VS Code detects that you are using Python, it will prompt to load appropriate extensions for you. You should allow it to do this as, once it knows about Python, it will be able to help you write the code by highlighting problems in the code and offering to remind you of the names of variables and functions (amongst other things).

django

There are many frameworks for creating web applications. Probably the most popular option for Python developers is *django*. As these things go, django has the advantage that it is fairly quick and easy to get started. It also has a Python-friendly database and a Python-based web server that will be fine for experimenting with, although neither should be used for large-scale deployment as they are not designed to cope with large numbers of simultaneous users.

If you have been working through the book in order, then you will have already installed django in Chapter 7. If you haven't yet installed django, head back to Chapter 7 for instructions on doing this.

You can check that django is correctly installed by running the following command, which should show a list of options:

```
> python -m django

Type 'django-admin help <subcommand>' for help on a specific
    subcommand.

Available subcommands:

[django]
    check
    compilemessages
    createcachetable
    ...
```

Creating a django Project

Having successfully installed django, it's time to create a new django project for our example. In this chapter, we will build up the example a step at a time. You will run commands from the command line and edit code. The final result of this effort is included in the book's downloads (see Page 34) in the folder called *django*.

We will use django's command line interface (CLI). But, before issuing the command we need to change directory to the directory where you want the project files to be created. This, can just be your home directory, as all the project files will themselves be created in a folder within your chosen folder. So, in Windows Power Shell or the Linux or Mac Terminal, type the command below to change to your home directory.

```
> cd ~
```

The squiggly line is the tilda key – on a Windows US keyboard, this can be found near the Enter key, and on a Mac keyboard between the left shift-key and the Z key.

You may be pleased to learn that a lot of the code for our django example project is going to be created for us by django itself. That is, when we enter the following command to create the django project, this will create Python and configuration files for us, as a starting point for our project. We can then use VS Code to edit this code and add new files as needed.

```
> python -m django startproject contacts_project
```

If you use VS Code to open the folder *contacts_project* that the command just created, you will see something like Figure 8.6.

Have a look around the files, but don't change anything just yet – and don't worry if it's not clear what everything does.

Creating a django App

A django project can contain multiple applications. So the next step is to use the django CLI to generate some more code for us in the form of the app itself, which we are going to call just *contacts*. Before issuing the command to create the app, make sure that you change directory into the project folder.

Figure 8.6. A new django project in VS Code.

```
> cd contacts_project
> python manage.py startapp contacts
```

Hop back to VS Code, and you should see that a new folder called contacts has been created, that contains a whole load of generated code files. Open the file *models.py* and you should see something like this:

```
from django.db import models

#Create your models here.
```

Referring back to Figure 8.3. the file *models.py* is where the ORM (Object Relational Mapping) lives. These are called *models* in django, and each model can be thought of as a Python version of a database table. We are going to write some Python to define a model that represents a person's contact details, and then use django's CLI to create the database table for us. So, finally, we get to write some code. Edit *models.py* so that it appears as below, and then save the changes to the file using *File, Save* (or CRTL-s on Windows and Linux and CMD-s on a Mac).

```
from django.db import models

# Create your models here.

class Contact(models.Model):
    first_name = models.CharField(max_length=100)
    surname = models.CharField(max_length=100)
    email = models.CharField(max_length=100)
    dob = models.DateField()
```

This code defines a new Python class called Contacts, that is a sub-class of models.Model. This subclassing allows Contacts to inherit all the database access code that the class Model knows how to do.

The Contacts class defines four attributes: first_name, surname and email are all defined as text strings (with a maximum size of 100 characters) and the dob field (date of birth) is defined as being a date field.

Before we can make use of this new code, we need to add a line to the project settings to tell the project about the contacts app, as this is one step that the app creation command does not do automatically. So open the file *settings.py* in the *contacts_project* folder and find the section that starts:

```
INSTALLED_APPS = [
```

Now add a line to the start of this list, so that that section of the code now appears as below.

```
INSTALLED_APPS = [
    'contacts.apps.ContactsConfig',
    'django.contrib.admin',
    'django.contrib.auth',
    'django.contrib.contenttypes',
    'django.contrib.sessions',
    'django.contrib.messages',
    'django.contrib.staticfiles',
]
```

The class ContactsConfig is in the file *contacts/apps.py* and was generated for us when we ran the command to create the app.

Creating a Database

The django CLI can read *models.py* and use it to update the database. Start by running the following command:

```
> python manage.py makemigrations contacts
Migrations for 'contacts':
  contacts/migrations/0001_initial.py
    - Create model Contact
```

This command is actually generating some Python code called a *migration* that, when run in a separate step, will actually make the changes to the database. Creating a file to change the database, rather than just changing the database, is a useful technique that allows the system to migrate from one version of the database structure (schema) to another. If you are curious, you can go and look at the migration code, which you will find in *contacts/migrations/0001_initial.py*. There is no need to edit this generated code but, to actually change the database, we need to run the migration using the command:

```
% python manage.py sqlmigrate contacts 0001
BEGIN;
--
-- Create model Contact
--
CREATE TABLE "contacts_contact" ("id" integer NOT NULL
    PRIMARY KEY AUTOINCREMENT, "first_name" varchar(100) NOT
    NULL, "surname" varchar(100) NOT NULL, "email"
    varchar(100) NOT NULL, "dob" date NOT NULL);
COMMIT;
```

This command has generated and run a database SQL command to create a database table called (a little redundantly) `contacts_contact`.

To bring the rest of the system up to date, we now need to issue a general migration command using:

```
> python manage.py migrate
Operations to perform:
  Apply all migrations: admin, auth, contacts, contenttypes,
    sessions
Running migrations:
```

```
Applying contenttypes.0001_initial... OK
Applying auth.0001_initial... OK
Applying admin.0001_initial... OK
Applying admin.0002_logentry_remove_auto_add... OK
Applying admin.0003_logentry_add_action_flag_choices... OK
Applying contenttypes.0002_remove_content_type_name... OK
Applying auth.0002_alter_permission_name_max_length... OK
Applying auth.0003_alter_user_email_max_length... OK
Applying auth.0004_alter_user_username_opts... OK
Applying auth.0005_alter_user_last_login_null... OK
Applying auth.0006_require_contenttypes_0002... OK
Applying auth.0008_alter_validators_add_error_messages... OK
Applying auth.0008_alter_user_username_max_length... OK
Applying auth.0009_alter_user_last_name_max_length... OK
Applying auth.0010_alter_group_name_max_length... OK
Applying auth.0011_update_proxy_permissions... OK
Applying auth.0012_alter_user_first_name_max_length... OK
Applying contacts.0001_initial... OK
Applying sessions.0001_initial... OK
```

So we now have a database – but, as yet, no data in it.

The django Admin Web Interface

The django system includes an administration interface that allows
us to do various things, including interacting with the ORM models
to add and modify data in the database. To do this, we have to first
create a *super-user* (full access) account on the database, using the
CLI command below:

```
> python manage.py createsuperuser
Username (leave blank to use 'user'): admin
Email address: none@email.com
Password:
Password (again):
This password is too common.
Bypass password validation and create user anyway? [y/N]: y
Superuser created successfully.
```

We are only playing, so it's forgivable to use utterly insecure credentials such as a username of *admin* and a password of *password*.

Before we can interact with our table of contacts, we need to change the file *contacts/admin.py,* to register our `Contact` model. Edit the file so that it appears as below:

```
from django.contrib import admin

# Register your models here.
from .models import Contact
admin.site.register(Contact)
```

You may have noticed that the import has a dot before `models`. This dot tells Python to look for the file to import in the current directory rather than being a standard module to import.

Save the changes and then run the following command:

```
> python manage.py runserver
Watching for file changes with StatReloader
Performing system checks...

System check identified no issues (0 silenced).
January 11, 2023 - 11:03:58
Django version 4.1.5, using settings
    'contacts_project.settings'
Starting development server at http://127.0.0.1:8000/
Quit the server with CONTROL-C.
```

As the response to the last command suggests, this has started a webserver running on your computer. So, open a browser tab and navigate to the URL shown: `http://127.0.0.1:8000/admin` You should then see a login screen like the one shown in Figure 8.7.

Enter the credentials you used earlier to create the super user and you should see something like Figure 8.8.

Options at the top allow you to manage users and groups but, for us, the interesting part is the *CONTACTS* section. Click on the *Add (+)* button and fill out the form (Figure 8.9) for the new contact, and then click on the *SAVE* button.

You may like to experiment, creating some new contacts for us to use as test data.

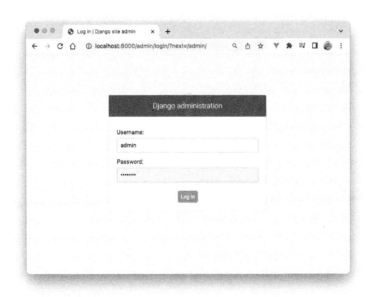

Figure 8.7. Logging into the django admin console.

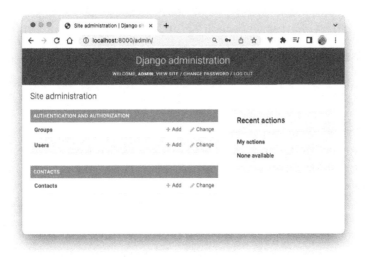

Figure 8.8. The Admin home page.

Making an API for Contacts

Just to recap, we now have a functioning system that allows us to use django's general purpose admin console to add and edit data in

129

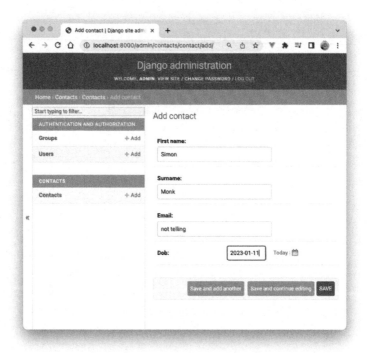

Figure 8.9. Creating a new contact using the django admin interface.

our contacts database. The next piece of work that we need to do is to create an API that will allow us to send a web request to get our list of contacts in JSON format.

We first met JSON back in Chapter 6. JSON is a way of representing objects (for example a contact) in a text format. We might represent a contact like this:

```
{
    "first_name": "Simon",
    "surname": "Monk",
    "email": "not telling",
    "dob": "2023-01-11"
}
```

To get such data from django requires us to effectively create a new web page which, when requested by a browser, will return a JSON list of objects representing the contacts in the database.

We will create the code for this web page in a new file within the contacts folder called *api.py*. To create the new file in VS Code, right-click while over the contacts folder and select the option *New File ...* Give the newly created file the name *api.py* and write the following code into it.

```python
from django.http import JsonResponse
from django.core import serializers
from contacts.models import Contact
import json


# Create your API calls here}

def list(request):
    contacts = Contact.objects.all()
    contacts_json = serializers.serialize('json', contacts)
    return JsonResponse(json.loads(contacts_json), safe=False)
```

There are various imports that we need, and then a function called list. The list function first fetches all of the contacts from the database. These objects are not, as you might expect, a Python List of Python Dictionary, but rather special classes that represent a database search result.

The list function then uses a serializer to convert this list of search result objects into a JSON string. However, the JsonResponse class expects a standard Python List of Dictionaries, and so json.loads (load string) is used to convert the string into this format. And yes – this is not at all efficient, its just how it is.

Before we can access this list api call, we need to configure both the *contacts* project and *contacts app* to be aware of it. First, create a new file in *contacts* called *urls.py* and put the following code into it:

```python
from django.urls import path
from . import api

urlpatterns = [
    path('list', api.list, name='list'),
]
```

This sets up a URL path so that the list function will be called whenever the browser requests a page called *list* within contacts. But this won't work just yet, because we haven't told the contacts project to also look at urls that the contacts app knows about. To do that, edit the file *contacts_project/urls.py* so that the code part looks like this:

```python
from django.contrib import admin
from django.urls import include, path

urlpatterns = [
    path('admin/', admin.site.urls),
    path('contacts/', include('contacts.urls')),
]
```

Save the changes and open a new browser tab at `http://127.0.0.1:8000/contacts/list` and you will see the JSON data for any contacts that you created (Figure 8.10).

Figure 8.10. The contacts list API call from a browser.

Try adding some more contacts, using the admin interface, and then refresh the page. Let's reformat the JSON in Figure 2.4, by spreading it out onto multiple lines, so we can see the structure a bit better.

```
[
    {
        "model": "contacts.contact",
        "pk": 1,
```

```
        "fields": {
            "first_name": "Simon",
            "surname": "Monk",
            "email": "not telling",
            "dob": "2023-01-11"
        }
    },
    {
        "model": "contacts.contact",
        "pk": 2,
        "fields": {
            "first_name": "Linda",
            "surname": "Monk",
            "email": "none",
            "dob": "2023-01-11"
        }
    }
]
```

The outer square brackets show us that a JSON list has been re-turned. Within this list, there are two JSON objects, representing each of the two contacts. Each of these contact objects has three parts.

- model (contacts.contact) that tells us what type of object we have

- pk (primary key) the internal database key for that contact row on the database table

- fields – The actual data about the contact, including first_name, surname, email and dob.

For a real system we would also need API calls to create, update and delete contacts but, for the sake of keeping this example relatively straight-forward, let's stop here and say that we have now completed the back-end of our system. We have a functioning database and an API that allows us to retrieve data from the database using a web request. The next step is to create a front end to access these contact details.

HTML

When Tim Bernes-Lee invented the world wide web, what he really invented was the HTML (HyperText Markup Language) – a text format that allowed you to create a web page to be displayed in a browser window. Most of the HTML was concerned with how the page looked, so `<h1>Heading</h1>` would display everything between `<h1>` and `</h1>` in a large bold font, so that you can tell its a heading. Normal paragraph text would be contained between a `<p>` and a `</p>`.

Other tags would be responsible for displaying forms or including images or linking to other web pages.

By kind permission of commitstrip.com

Web pages still contain HTML, but now generally also contain two other things mixed in with the HTML.

- Style sheets that fine tune the appearance of the web page, so that instead of all h1 headings looking the same, you can change every aspect of the layout and appearance of any tag.

- Script tags that contain code in the JavaScript programming language. These can do anything from simple validation of input fields, to making web requests in the background that then modify what is displayed on the browser.

A modern web page will load once, when you go to that page, and then use JavaScript to modify what is displayed on the page. Effectively web pages have changed from being just content for display into programs in their own right.

Vue and Bootstrap

Now that the original egalitarian concept of all web pages having much the same vanilla appearance has been thrown out of the window, there is an onus on the programmer to make web pages look aesthetically nice. This is a skill often lacking in the programmer's toolset. However, fortunately, we can make use of other people's work to make our web pages look nice and interface well with APIs to access the data they need.

For our rudimentary user interface we will make use of two frameworks:

- Vue – a JavaScript framework to help us manage the active logic of our web page, such as requesting data, and do things like running JavaScript functions when a button is pressed, or looping over each of the contacts to display each in turn.

- Bootstrap – a stylesheet framework to make everything look good.

The way we are going to use both Vue and Bootstrap is to simply add code in our web page to download them into the browser from an internet server somewhere, and then use them directly. This works, but it's not very efficient, and a real live system would not be deployed in this way.

We are doing it this way because the recommended way of using Vue in particular is very powerful, but also very complex, and a full treatment of such a process would be a book in its own right.

Creating a Default Page Template

We will start by creating a basic web page that can act as the starting point for our web interface. This page would not normally need to have anything to do with django. In fact it would normally be served by a web server. But, rather than run a separate web server, we are going to let jango host this page.

Start by opening the file *contacts/views* and adding a new method called `index` as shown below.

```
from django.shortcuts import render

# Create your views here.

def index(request):
    return render(request, 'index.html')
```

This `index` function says that when it is called in response to a request from a browser, it is to serve up the contents of a file called *index.html* (which we haven't created yet). So let's create *index.html*. This needs to be inside a folder called *templates* in *contacts*, so create a new folder by right clicking on the *contacts* folder and selecting *New Folder...* and then create the new file in that folder called *index.html* and place the following text in it.

```
<h1>This is index.html</h1>
```

There are now a couple of configuration changes that we need to make so that the django web server can find the template that we have just created. First of all edit *contacts_project/settings.py* and find the section that starts:

```
TEMPLATES = [
```

in the DIRS section of this file add a string for the templates folder that we created earlier, so that the section looks like this:

```
TEMPLATES = [
    {
        'BACKEND': 'django.template.backends.django.DjangoTemplates',
        'DIRS': ['templates'],
        'APP_DIRS': True,
        'OPTIONS': {
            'context_processors': [
                'django.template.context_processors.debug',
                'django.template.context_processors.request',
                'django.contrib.auth.context_processors.auth',
```

```
        'django.contrib.messages.context_processors.messages',
      ],
    },
  },
]
```

We also need to revisit *urls.py* in *contacts* (not to be confused with
the one in the *project* folder) and add a line for the new path for
index. Note that an import for views has also been added to the file.

```
from django.urls import path
from . import views
from . import api

urlpatterns = [
    path('', views.index, name='index'),
    path('list', api.list, name='list'),
]
```

Now open a browser tab on http://127.0.0.1:8000/contacts/
and you should see the content shown in Figure 8.12.

Figure 8.12. A basic page served by django.

A Vue and Bootstrap Front-end

Now that we have django serving a basic web page from the file *index.html* for us, we can change that file to provide us with a Vue and Bootstrap user interface.

Now is a good time to switch from typing code into VS Code and either download the example project, or copy and paste the code from github (`https://github.com/simonmonk/coding_book`)

The code for the Vue page looks a bit daunting, but much of it is what's called *boiler plate code* – that is, code that stays the same whatever the page is doing. This is the sort of code that developers will not normally write from scratch. They are more likely to copy a basic template page, and then change it to contain the bits they need that are specific to their application.

Here is the basic structure, with some comments by way of explanation. Note that comments in HTML are contained between <!-- and --> and, in Javascript, anything after // until the end of the line is treated as a comment:

```
{% verbatim %}   <!-- required by django for formatting reasons -->
<!DOCTYPE html>. <!-- indicates to a prowser that this is an HTML page -->
<html>           <!-- The whole web page contents should be enclosed in an <html> tag -->

<head>
    <meta charset="utf-8" />   <!-- Use Unicode 8 bit, as the content is only Roman fonts -->
    <title>Contacts</title>    <!-- This will appear as the page title in it's browser tab -->

    <!-- Imports of Vue, Bootstrap and any other JavaScript libraries needed goes here -->
</head>

<body>
    <div id="vapp">
    <!-- HTML containing extra Vue commands goes here -->
    </div>

    <script>
        var app = new Vue({
            el: '#vapp',
            data: {
                // Any data structures used by Vue goes here
            },
            mounted: function () {
                // This is where you put code to be called when the page loads
            },
            methods: {
                // define functions here to be used by the Vue framework
                // - for example to call an API and change data being displayed
            }
        });
    </script>
</body>

</html>
{% endverbatim %}
```

Here is the actual code, with the parts specific to this application added into the structure.

```
{% verbatim %}
<!DOCTYPE html>
<html>

<head>
    <meta charset="utf-8" />
    <title>Contacts</title>
    <meta name="viewport" content="width=device-width, initial-scale=1, shrink-to-fit=no">
    <link rel="stylesheet"
        href="https://cdn.jsdelivr.net/npm/bootstrap@4.3.1/dist/css/bootstrap.min.css"
        integrity="sha384-ggOyR0iXCbMQv3Xipma34MD+dH/1fQ784/j6cY/iJTQUOhcWr7x9JvoRxT2MZw1T"
        crossorigin="anonymous">
    <script src="https://cdn.jsdelivr.net/npm/vue/dist/vue.js"></script>
</head>

<body>
    <div id="vapp">
        <h1>Contacts</h1>

        <div class="list-group">
            <a v-for="contact in contacts" class="list-group-item list-group-item-action">
                <div class="d-flex w-100 justify-content-between">
                    <h5 class="mb-1">{{contact.fields.first_name}} {{contact.fields.surname}}</h5>
                </div>
                <p class="mb-1">{{contact.fields.email}} {{contact.fields.dob}}</p>
            </a>
        </div>
        <div>
            <button class="btn btn-primary" v-on:click="load_items">Refresh</button>
        </div>
    </div>

    <script>
        var app = new Vue({
            el: '#vapp',
            data: {
                contacts: []
            },
            mounted: function () {
                this.load_items();
            },
            methods: {
                load_items: function () {
                    const xhr = new XMLHttpRequest();
                    xhr.open("GET", "/contacts/list");
                    xhr.send();
                    xhr.responseType = "json";
                    xhr.onload = () => {
                        if (xhr.readyState == 4 && xhr.status == 200) {
                            const data = xhr.response;
                            this.contacts = data;
                        } else {
                            console.log(\lstinline`Error: ${xhr.status}`);
                        }
                    };
                },
            }
        });
    </script>
</body>

</html>
{% endverbatim %}
```

The {% verbatim %} tags around the whole file tell django's template mechanism not to try and substitute any values into the template file.

The next section, inside the <head> tag, imports the Bootstrap style

139

sheet and Vue JavaScript. Inside the `<body>` tag you will find a `<div>` tag with an id of `vapp` (Vue app). This tag contains the actual user interface HTML elements that Vue will interact with. This starts with a `<h1>` tag containing the text *Contacts*. It then has a `<div>` tag with a class of `list-group`. This will contain the list of contacts.

The `<a>` tag contains an attribute 'v-for="contact in contacts"' that will iterate for each `contact` in turn. The different parts of the contact are displayed using the `{{ }}` notation.

At the end of the vapp `<div>` tag is the refresh button. This has an attribute `v-on:click="load_items"`. This will call the `load_items` function when the button is clicked.

After the vapp `<div>` tag is a `<script>` tag that contains the JavaScript used to make the Vue app work. The `el` attribute has a value of `#vapp` to link the code to the vapp `<div>` tag. The app must be structured with sections of `data`, `mounted` and `methods`. The `data` section contains any data that the Vue app uses. In this case that's just a list of contacts. The `mounted` section contains code that will be run when the page is loaded. In this case, that just means calling the `load_items` method from the next section.

The `load_items` method uses JavaScript's built-in `XMLHttpRequest` class to send a web request to */contacts/list*, that brings back the JSON for the contacts and assigns it to the variable `contacts`.

To take a look at this in action refresh your browser tab on the page http://127.0.0.1:8000/contacts/

The result should look like Figure 8.13. Try adding some more contacts in the Admin interface, and clicking on the Refresh button on the web page.

Note that the Refresh button modifies the data shown in the page without reloading the page from the web server. This is a subtle but important distinction, because it means that you won't see a blink as the page reloads – only the data is fetched, not the entire page.

Summary

We have covered a lot of ground in this chapter, and if you have followed along, building up the applications, you should now have a

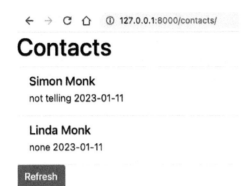

Figure 8.13. A Vue web interface for Contacts.

fair idea of what full-stack development is like.

In the next chapter, we will survey some of the other programming languages and get a flavour of how different they are from Python.

9

Other Languages

In this chapter we will take a look at some of the other popular programming languages. We will look at how they differ from Python, and what advantages they may offer. By necessity, this will only be an overview of the languages – and in some cases offer a few examples to experiment with, but we will not attempt to learn these languages here.

JavaScript

We saw some JavaScript in Chapter 8, where we used the Vue framework (written in JavaScript) to provide a web front-end for our example project. JavaScript is included as part of modern browsers and so is the natural choice for code that runs in the browser. As programming languages go, JavaScript is a bit of a dog's breakfast. It has many ways of accomplishing the same thing leading to code that is often hard to follow. One initiative to tame JavaScript and make it easier to maintain is TypeScript. This is compatible with JavaScript, but adds a layer on top of JavaScript that allows type checking, to make it more robust.

In Chapter 8, we used JavaScript running in the browser, however, JavaScript can also be used on a server. The platform usually used for this is *Node.js*. Node.js fulfils the same role that django and Python did for us in Chapter 8. It includes its own package manager

143

Figure 9.1. By kind permission of commitstrip.com

(npm) for installing software and has its own CLI for generating code.

Installing Node.js is a good way to play with JavaScript from the command line, as we have done with the Python Shell. You can install Node.js using the instructions and downloads from `https://nodejs.org/en/download/`.

Having installed Node.js, you can open a console or shell, and type command as you would in Python.

```
% node
Welcome to Node.js v18.12.1.
Type ".help" for more information.
> 2+2
4
>
```

Some of the early Python examples, such as creating and accessing lists, will work just the same in JavaScript. For example:

```
> titles = ['Jaws', 'The Godfather', 'Baby Driver', 'Inception']
[ 'Jaws', 'The Godfather', 'Baby Driver', 'Inception' ]
> titles[3]
> 'Inception'
```

One of the main differences between Python and JavaScript is that
JavaScript does not use indentation for blocks of code. Instead, like
many languages, it uses curly braces ({}). Even though curly braces
are used instead of indentation, it's still a good idea to indent text
within a block.

Also, instead of the word `def` to mark the start of a function definition, JavaScript uses the word `function`.

Listing: javascript/09_01_polite_function.js

```
function make_polite(sentence) {
  polite_sentence = sentence + ' please';
  return polite_sentence;
}

console.log(make_polite('Pass the salt'))
```

Instead of `print`, JavaScript uses the `console.log` method to display
text.

As with many languages, JavaScript and Python have more in common than they have different, and if you are learning a new language,
it's mostly a case of finding out how you do X in the new language.
As with so many things, an internet search will often give you the
answer quite quickly.

Java

JavaScript and Java are not at all closely related – at best, they are
distant cousins in the family tree of programming languages. Java
is the older language and while it does have a superficially similar
syntax (using curly braces for blocks of code for example), Java is a
strongly-typed language. That is, when you declare a variable, you
have to specify the type of the variable – whether its a string, or

integer etc.

Unlike Python or JavaScript, having specified the type, you cannot then use that variable to hold any other type. Java has a more heavy-weight reputation and can be somewhat verbose to read.

At one time, Java was the most-used programming language but, in recent years, has lost ground to lighter-weight languages like Python and JavaScript.

Java does not have a shell with which to interact. The source code is built or compiled into byte code (a form suitable for running) without having an interactive element.

C# (pronounced C Sharp) is Microsoft's take on Java, and very similar.

C++

C++ is the object-oriented extension of the C programming language. First released in 1972 by Dennis Ritchie, C++ has gradually added features on top of features to keep pace with new ideas in software development.

When written well, C and C++ can be extremely fast and are often used in software libraries for computationally intensive applications like machine learning and computer vision, where performance is at a premium. In fact, it's not uncommon to find Python wrappers to C++ code that use Python as the easy-to-use interface and let the C++ do the heavy lifting.

C++ is another compiled language, and so does not have a shell. The source code is compiled directly into the binary code to be run on the computer. Being *close to the metal* is what provides C++ with its high performance.

Ruby on Rails

The django framework is very much inspired by Ruby on Rails. Ruby is the programming language and Rails is the web framework, rather like Python and django.

Rails has most of the same ideas as django – you create projects and generate migrations etc from the CLI and it has models, that map objects to a relational database with a minimum of fuss.

As a language, Ruby is a much purer object-oriented language than Python. Ruby has a very permissive syntax. For example, the parentheses around function parameters are optional so, to print the string hello, you can write:

```
puts('hello')
```

or

```
puts 'hello'
```

... both will work – but many purists consider this to be a bad thing, preferring a language to make its mind up and just offer one way of doing something.

Ruby has equivalents of Python *lists* and *dictionaries* that it calls *arrays* and *hashes* respectively. So, our list of movie hashes from back in Chapter 3 could be written, as shown in the following listing, in Ruby.

This code also prints out the three titles. You can find the program in *09_01_list_of_hashes.rb* within the ruby folder of the book's downloads and is the direct equivalent of the python program *03_04_list_dict.py*.

Listing: 09_01_list_of_hashes.rb

```
movies = [
    {
        'title' => 'Jaws',
        'director' => 'Steven Spielberg',
        'duration'=> 124
    },
    {
        'title' => 'The Godfather',
        'director' => 'Francis Ford Coppola,',
        'duration' => 175
    },
    {
        'title' => 'Baby Driver',
        'director' => 'Edgar Wright',
        'duration' => 115
```

```
    }
]

movies.each do | movie |
    puts(movie['title'])
end
```

The code is actually very similar to its Python equivalent. The main differences are that:

- keys and values are separated by => rather than :

- iterating over the array uses the .each method.

Whereas blocks of code in Python are indicated by indentation, in Ruby you get a choice. You can either use do and end, like we did in the example above, or curly braces { and } – so the code at the end of the example above could also be written as:

```
movies.each { | movie |
    puts(movie['title'])
}
```

Cool Languages

The languages described above are all popular languages, and are good languages to know from a career point of view. However, if you get into programming, you might like to try one of the languages below.

Smalltalk

The majority of the popular languages that describe themselves as object-oriented are based on non-object-oriented languages. Smalltalk was one of the first true object-oriented languages, where absolutely everything is an object (an instance of a class). Even things like conditional (if) statements are treated as objects. For example, here is some Smalltalk code that compares a number with a variable, and prints a message if something is true.

```
(x > 10)
    ifTrue: [ Transcript show: 'x is big' ].
```

Beyond this slightly odd looking syntax, almost the only thing that's pure Smalltalk language (rather than built-in objects and methods) are the brackets – let me explain.

First of all, just to make the comparison, x is a variable (expected to be an instance of a number class of some sort, that understands the > method with a parameter of a second number (in this case 10). The > method returns an instance of the Boolean class. The boolean class has two subclasses, True and False, and each of these classes has a method called ifTrue that takes, as its parameter, a block of code (square brackets) to be run. True's ifTrue method will run the code, whereas False's ifTrue method will do nothing.

What's more, the development environment for creating Smalltalk code is a fundamental part of Smalltalk itself. Smalltalk does not have source code files – you just edit methods on classes, one at a time, in their own editor window.

There are now several free Smalltalk systems. Figure 9.2 shows the Squeak Smalltalk system that you can download from https://squeak.org/.

Figure 9.2. Editing a method in SmallTalk

You write your program by adding your own classes and methods, or adding your own methods to existing classes. Built-in classes are treated no differently from the classes you create.

So the class Browser in Figure 9.2 shows the class hierarchy around the Boolean logic classes, as you can see, `False` and `True` are subclases of `Boolean`, which is a subclass of `Object`, which is itself a subclass of `ProtoObject`. All of this code is completely accessible to the programmer.

Aside from a few niche applications, where the ability to modify programs quickly (such as trading desks and some other financial applications), Smalltalk is now used very little. Its lack of free or even low-cost versions in its early years, and its radical approach, probably sealed its fate – but it is a language much loved by those of us who have used it.

LISP/Scheme/Clojure

LISP (LISt Processing) and its newer incarnations of Scheme, Clojure and, to some extent, JavaScript are *functional* programming languages. Most languages have functions of some sort, but in pure functional languages, the only variables are local variables and functions are not allowed to have *side effects* – that is, to affect any variables that are not within the function.

LISP is one of the oldest functional languages (1960) and uses round brackets to denote the content of a list, where the first element of the list might be a function or operator name followed by parameters.

In LISP, lists are not just data structures, the code itself is contained in lists. So you end up with a lot of brackets in LISP programs.

For example, to add 2 and 2 you would write.

```
(+ 2 2)
4
```

You can try this out online by visiting `https://common-lisp.net/downloads` and clicking on the *Try Online* button. This opens the equivalent of the Python shell, but for LISP.

LISP does have a built-in list-reversing function, but as an example, let's look at how we could implement this in LISP.

```
(defun rev (list)
  (let ((return-value))
    (dolist (e list) (push e return-value))
    return-value))
```

You can try this out in the LISP shell (Figure 9.3).

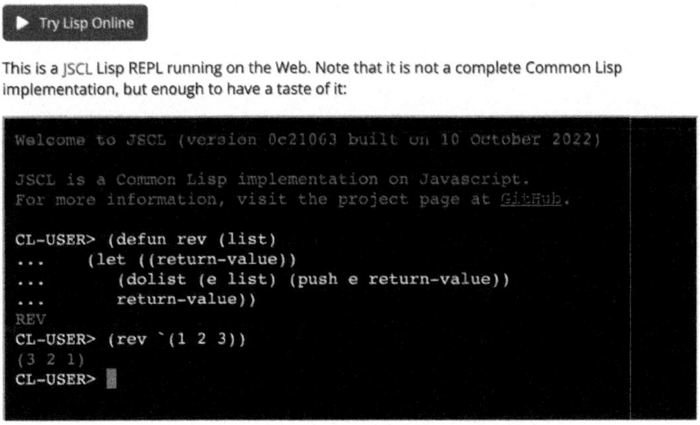

Figure 9.3. Interactive LISP

Functions are defined using **defun**, which is followed by the function name and parameters. Note that, in LISP, everything is a list enclosed in (and), even the code. Unlike Python, and many other languages, items in a list are not separated by commas.

The **let** function is LISP's way of assigning values to variables. After **let** the local variable name is specified (return-value) and then value. This value is, in this case, code to be run using the local variable. This code uses the **dolist** iterator that pushes values onto return-value. As the last thing in the function return-value is returned by the function. Notice that LISP is one of the few programming languages that will let you include a - in a variable name.

In recent years, functional languages have become popular again, largely thanks to the influence of JavaScript.

Summary

Once you have learnt one language, getting started with another is relatively easy. Apart from the more exotic languages, the basic

151

concepts are the same, but the syntax and commands used vary. It's often harder learning, say, a new web framework than the underlying language.

Part II.

Working in Software

10

Software Engineering

If programming is construction, then software engineering is civil engineering. There is a lot more to a successful software project than enthusiastic developers. Everyone needs to be on the same page and have a common vision of exactly what the project is trying to accomplish and how it will be implemented.

In this chapter, we will explore the topic of software engineering, looking at the different approaches to developing software and, along the way, learn a bit more about what software development teams do.

Methodologies

Organisations all have their own way of working and doing things, that evolves in directions dictated by the people who run and work in the business. This is nowhere more obvious than in how they carry out their software development.

For a long time, the software industry has struggled to come up with a reliable way for a big team to produce software. Traditionally this would have been the *waterfall model* where requirements were devised quite separately from the process of actually coding. However, in recent years, software development has become a more collaborative activity, with the *business* and *developers* working together more closely.

By kind permission of commitstrip.com

Software development processes are often formalised by software gurus. With the promise of solving an organisation's software development problems at one stroke these software development methodologies are often comercialized with books and training courses and certification for developers.

Waterfall

The waterfall model is a traditional approach to software development that proceeds in steps. It consists of several stages, each of which must be completed before the next one can begin:

1. Design: The *design* phase involves creating a detailed plan for making the software – including designs for classes, software modules, interfaces, and algorithms.

2. Requirements gathering: This first stage involves gathering and documenting all the requirements for the software project. This includes understanding the user needs, defining the scope of the project, and creating a detailed project plan.

3. Implementation: The implementation phase involves actually

writing and testing the code for each part of the software, and then integrating them into a complete system.

4. Testing: The testing phase involves verifying that the software meets all the requirements, is free of bugs, and is reliable.

5. Deployment: The final stage involves delivering the finished software to the users.

This approach is often used for large, complex software projects that require a detailed plan and a clear set of requirements. However, the downside of the waterfall model is that it can be slow and inflexible, and it doesn't always allow for changes or revisions to the software during the development process.

In practice, organisations that primarily use a waterfall process will generally have their own take on it, perhaps introducing their own ways of making waterfall more interactive with the business.

Agile

Agile software development is an iterative and incremental approach to software development that encourages flexibility, collaboration, and customer satisfaction.

The Agile methodology involves breaking down the software development process into small, iterative, cycles sometimes called *sprints*, each of which produces a working piece of software that can be reviewed and tested by the team and the customer.

Agile development is based on the Agile Manifesto, a set of principles that prioritize as follows:

1. Individuals and interactions over processes and tools

2. Working software over comprehensive documentation

3. Customer collaboration over contract negotiation

4. Responding to change over following a plan

The Agile methodology typically involves a small team that works together to deliver a working software product in short cycles. The team meets regularly to discuss progress, identify any obstacles, and adjust the plan as necessary. Agile development also emphasizes the importance of continuous feedback from customers, which is used to refine the product and make adjustments to the development process.

Agile development is often used for projects that require frequent changes, or when the requirements are not well-defined at the beginning of the project. It allows for greater flexibility, adaptability, and responsiveness to changes in customer needs and market conditions, making it a popular choice for software development in many industries.

As with waterfall-based methodologies, agile methodologies have also become productized. Scrum is one of the most popular of these methodologies, with ready availability of training courses and other training material.

The Scrum team consists of three roles: the Product Owner, the Scrum Master, and the Development Team. The Product Owner is responsible for defining the product backlog, which is a prioritized list of features and requirements that the team will work on. The Scrum Master is responsible for facilitating the Scrum process and ensuring that the team is following the framework. The Development Team is responsible for delivering the product incrementally and iteratively.

The Scrum methodology comprises a series of events:

- Sprint Planning is the time when the team decides what they will work on during the upcoming sprint.

- The Daily Scrum is a short, daily meeting where the team discusses their progress and plans for the day. This is usually a *stand-up* meeting, to stop people getting too physically comfortable and making the meeting longer than it needs to be.

- The Sprint Review is a meeting where the team demonstrates the work they have completed, during the sprint, to stakeholders.

- The Sprint Retrospective is a meeting where the team reflects on the previous sprint and identifies areas for improvement and the next sprint.

UML (Unified Modeling Language)

UML diagrams are used to communicate the design of software systems to stakeholders such as developers, testers, project managers, and business analysts. UML helps to visualize the different aspects of a system, which makes it easier to understand and analyze the design. It also helps to identify potential problems or issues in the system design before implementation.

UML has many different types of diagram, for expressing many ideas about software design, including the following – two of which are discussed in more detail below.

- Class diagrams.

- Component diagrams.

- Use case diagrams.

- Sequence diagrams.

If you are using a waterfall model, then UML diagrams will find their way into the often large volume of documentation that accompany the software development process. In more agile settings, UML diagrams are more likely to be temporary, and appear on a whiteboard as a vehicle for achieving a common understanding of a part of a design, or discussing some tricky aspect of the implementation. Such diagrams might not be incorporated into a document, but might be photographed as a reminder.

Programmers are often visual thinkers, and a good diagram is a great way of communicating how something is used or how it can be coded. While UML provides a fairly exact definition of how different types of drawing should be made, in reality these diagrams are often simplified and less formal.

Let's take a look at a couple of the most common UML diagrams.

Use Case Diagrams

Use case diagrams are a good way of expressing who is going to be using a system and what they are going to be doing with it. For example, Figure 10.2 shows an example use case for a movie database example.

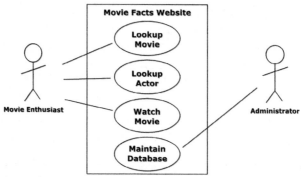

Figure 10.2. A Use Case diagram for a movie database website.

In this simplified example, we are showing just a couple of types of user – the end user of the database that we have called the Movie Enthusiast and the Administrator who maintains the system. From the use cases, we can decide on what user interfaces are going to be required.

Sequence Diagrams

Sequence diagrams are a good way of expressing complex sequences of actions occurring in a system. We saw a kind of simplified sequence diagram in Figure 7.4 which is repeated here as Figure 10.3.

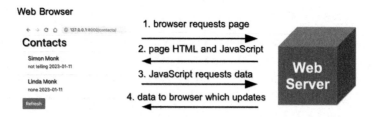

Figure 10.3. A simplified sequence diagram.

This version of a sequence diagram is somewhat informal and simplified, in comparison to UML's definition of a sequence diagram, but it serves well as a way of explaining the interactions involved in the different parts of the system.

Developers collect and even develop their own types of diagram as a way of communicating with users and other developers.

Source Code Management

Every developer will have a *machine* that they use to carry out their programming tasks. People will be working on the same system, each working away on their own copy of the code, so how does all the code come back together properly. Where, if you like, does the master copy of the code live? The answer is that the reference copy is stored in a source code repository or *repo* which is a little like a database for source code. A dedicated computer or a cloud service will host the source code management software, and each developer will interact with the repo.

As anyone who has worked on a spreadsheet or word processor document on a shared network drive knows, there is always a risk that person A opens a document and starts working on it, and a second person B opens the same document and makes their changes. Person A might save their changes and close the document, thinking their work was safe, only for person B to then save their work, overwriting the work of person A.

When people first started using source code repositories, to prevent such over-writing of changes the repos used *pessimistic* concurrency control. That is, a developer would check out a file from the repo to make their changes, and no one else could change that file until the developer had *checked it in* again. This never worked very well, because inevitably developers would forget to check things back in when they had finished, or several developers needed to work on the same file at the same time, and one would have to wait.

These days, modern code repositories (of which *git* is the most popular) use *optimistic* concurrency control. That is, there is no locking of files but, instead, when one developer comes to *push* their changes, the repo software attempts to merge their changes with the master copy or *head* of the code.

For example if two developers are working on the same file, but different methods within that file, then there is little reason why their changes should overlap, and the software should be able to automatically *merge* their changes. However, if the repo software does spot such a *conflict*, and is unable to do a merge of the code, then it will flag (to the person trying to commit their code) that there is a problem that they need to go and sort out with the other developer.

Software like git that manages access to the repo also provides what is called version control. At its most granular, this happens as a new version of a file being created every time a change is committed. This means that you can always go back in time and see all the earlier versions of a file. This is very useful if someone makes a mistake and needs to revert to an earlier version of some code.

Version control can also be more specific, providing formally named releases of a whole repository – for example, when the code reaches a stable state ready to be released to people other than the developers.

Another extremely powerful concept in version control software like git is *branches*. This allows developers to branch off from the master copy of the code to work on a particular problem and then, when the work on that branch is complete, to merge it back into the master copy or *head*.

All of this branching and merging is much safer when accompanied by automated tests (see the next section), as these will quickly highlight any merge problems.

Unit Testing

One problem that occurs when you have a team of developers working on the same system is that one developer might change some code for their programming task that breaks some other piece of code that someone else wrote.

One way to guard against this problem is to write automated *unit tests* at the same time as you add features to the system. You can then, at any time, or especially after making a change, issue a command to run all the unit tests for the system.

They are called *unit tests*, because they are specific to a unit of the system rather than other types of test such as *integration tests* and *system tests* that test the software as a whole. All of these can be automated and help to provide confidence for developers to remove code that might be unused, or refactor common code to keep the code neat, and stave off the ravages of *code rot* as the code becomes larger and more unwieldy.

Most languages, including Python, have a unit testing framework. In fact there is often a choice of unit testing frameworks. Python has a built-in unit test framework called *PyUnit*.

The `Deck` class that we developed in Chapter 6 for our Blackjack game is just crying out for some unit tests.

```python
from card import Card
from random import shuffle

class Deck:

    def __init__(self):
        self.cards = []
        for suit in Card.possible_suits:
            for pips in Card.possible_pips:
                self.cards.append(Card(pips, suit))

    def __repr__(self):
        return '<Deck: ' + str(self.cards) + '>'

    def shuffle(self):
        shuffle(self.cards)

    def deal(self, n, hand):
        for i in range(0, n):
            hand.append(self.cards.pop())
```

In the file *06_card_game/deck_unit_tests.py* you will find some unit tests for the `Deck` class. To run the tests, just run the program *06_card_game/deck_unit_tests.py*.

Listing: 06_card_game/deck_unit_tests.py

```python
import unittest
from deck import Deck

class TestDeck(unittest.TestCase):

    def test_init(self):
        d = Deck()
        self.assertEqual(len(d.cards), 52, "incorrect number of cards")

    def test_deal(self):
        d = Deck()
        hand = []
        d.deal(3, hand)
        self.assertEqual(len(d.cards), 49, "incorrect deck size after dealing")
        self.assertEqual(len(hand), 3, "incorrect hand size after dealing")

unittest.main()
```

Having imported `unittest` and the `Deck` class from `deck`, a class called `TestDeck` is defined as a subclass of `unittest.TestCase`. Any methods starting with *test* in your class will automatically be run when the method `main` of `unittest` is called. In this case, there are two tests:

- `test_init` - tests that after a new `Deck` is created, it has 52 cards in it.

- `test_deal` - tests that after 3 cards are dealt to a hand, the hand contains 3 cards, and the deck is smaller by 3 cards.

These tests both use the `assertEqual` method that they inherit from `TestCase`. The first two parameters of this method are two values to be compared. Here, the values to be compared are numbers of cards, but they could be strings or any other type. The third parameter is a message to be displayed along with any test failure that occurs if the assertion fails.

As well as `assertEqual`, PyUnit has a whole lot of other types of assertion that can be used. You can read about them here: `https://docs.python.org/3/library/unittest.html`.

Try loading and running *06_card_game/deck_unit_tests.py*. You should see something like this:

```
>>> %Run deck_unit_tests.py
..
----
Ran 2 tests in 0.012s

OK

Process ended with exit code 0.
```

We can see what it looks like if a test fails, by deliberately sabotaging the code in *deck.py* on line 19, from:

```
for i in range(0, n):
```

to:

```
for i in range(1, n):
```

Re-run the tests and you should see something like this:

```
>>> %Run deck_unit_tests.py
F.
=================================================================
FAIL: test_deal (__main__.TestDeck)
Traceback (most recent call last):
  File "/Users/si/Dropbox/Books in progress/50
        Coding/code/coding_book/python/06_card_game/deck_unit_tests.py", line 14, in test_deal
    self.assertEqual(len(d.cards), 49, "incorrect deck size after dealing")
AssertionError: 50 != 49 : incorrect deck size after dealing
Ran 2 tests in 0.001s

FAILED (failures=1)
```

Don't forget to change the code back to fix the test.

Some software teams practice Test Driven Development (TDD). In TDD you would write the tests for a class like Deal before actually writing the code for Deal itself. In a way, the tests are specifying how the code should work, and you know you have completed your task when all the tests pass.

Exercises

The following exercises will give you a chance to add some more unit tests to the Blackjack example from Chapter 6. You can find model solutions to the exercises with the book downloads in the *exercise_solutions* folder and in Appendix B.

Exercise 10-1

Add another test for the deal method, that checks that when one card is dealt the card is no longer in the deck.

Hint: PyUnit has a assertNotIn method.

Exercise 10-2

Write a test for the shuffle method.

Hint: This is difficult, because of the random nature of the shuffle method. But a reasonable test might be to have two decks, one shuffled and one not. Then compare the cards before and after shuffling and make sure that no more than 5 of them are at the same place in the deck. You may find assertLess useful.

Summary

In this chapter, we have explored the topic of Software Engineering and added to our Python expertise by writing a few unit tests. In the next chapter we will take a closer look at the types of role available in software development.

11

Careers in Software

There are many paths into software development and also many different types of job when you get there. In this chapter we will look at how people get into a software development career and what kind of roles there are within the industry.

Routes into a Software Job

A quick survey of most software teams will find a wide number of routes into their current job. Some, but by no means all, will have followed the obvious route of studying Computer Science (CS) at University, while others will have found their way into the team in quite different ways.

Employers will often look for people who can demonstrate an enthusiasm for coding. Especially when it comes to candidates without formal qualifications, coding projects carried out for fun, can be a valuable demonstration of your competence. A link to a github or gitlab page hosting your work can be an asset on your resume.

The Academic Route

When on the lookout for new developers, organisations of all sizes will compete for new graduates in CS. These candidate employees have many advantages – in general they will be:

- intelligent and quick to learn

- enthusiastic

- skilled in programming

- able to bring new ideas into the organisation

- have specific valuable skills such as an understanding of machine learning

- be able to work from first principals with a theoretical backing. But this may lead them to try to *reinvent the wheel*

They may also come with a few potential disadvantages:

- no valuable team working skills

- poor engineering discipline (not used to the diligence required for professional software engineering)

- an over-inflated view of their own ability – only occasionally

Universities now offer Computing courses in an a variety of flavours to suit different types of student. Pure Computer Science courses are math heavy, but you will also find courses with a more practical or a business emphasis.

Having hired many people from this route, I can say that it works well when you are introducing such people into an established team, as they will pickup good software engineering discipline and the existing team will be exposed to the latest new ideas.

Academic Transfers

Many graduates of numerate disciplines, on completing their degrees, look around and find that there are a lot more jobs out there for developers than say Physicists or Chemists. What's more they will probably have taken programming courses. This is particularly true of Physicists who have the good fortune to have learnt programming and electronics as parts of their college courses.

Some may have moved onto a Masters degree to beef up their software skills. But in reality, however, such individuals don't need much conversion to make good developers.

Graduate Programs

Although less common than it used to be, large organisations (such as a big insurance company) sometimes have graduate programs, where they sweep up bright graduates from all sorts of disciplines and then invest considerable effort in showing the graduates all aspects of the business. Once *inducted*, the graduates can migrate towards roles in the organisation that suit or interest them – often moving into software development.

All necessary training is supplied by the organisation and the diversity of thought in teams constructed in this way often works well.

Home-Grown Talent

What I have written so far, might lead you to believe that a degree, whether in Computer Science or another subject, is a necessary requirement for a career in software. This is not the case. Most software teams will be all the better for including some members who have arrived through less academic routes.

For example, many large organisations, have talent programs, that allow employees with little in the way of academic qualifications to be plucked from say a retail store or call-centre into a development team, where their depth of product knowledge and ability to learn can be tested and often leads to permanent movement into software development roles.

The Prodigy

Programming can be an introspective skill, and it is not uncommon for teenagers to become extremely skilled in programming at a young age. Sometimes the talent of such people leads them into one of the academic routes described above, but other times, their obsession with this particular skill and other issues concerned with neuro-diversity mean that their general grades make the academic route difficult.

Some of these people will be picked up in the *Home-Grown Talent* route described earlier, but others will find their way into software roles through being *given a chance* by a friendly employer.

Getting that first foothold is the key, and a portfolio of projects and helpful friends and family can play a big part in securing that first job.

The Coding Interview

It is a foolish employer who hires on the basis of a candidates' word that they can program. The best way to find out, is to ask them to demonstrate this at interview, along with other skills that are needed for the role. Even a Computer Science degree does not always indicate that someone is good at coding.

The coding interview may include written tests, or working at a white board to demonstrate your thinking processes while working on a problem.

In both cases, no employer is going to be looking at exact precision in language syntax (that's what a good IDE will do for you). What they will be looking for is clarity of thought, and a methodical mind.

The results of Programming Aptitude Tests should be taken with large pinch of salt. I know an extremely capable programmer, with a doctorate in Computer Science, who failed the computing aptitude test for a large software consultancy.

Jobs in Software

Although people often start their careers writing code, they can migrate into other areas of software development that suit their personality or interests. They may become software testers, project managers or solutions architects.

Here are a selection of job titles that you might find in a software team. Transfers between these roles are very common.

Programmer/Developer

Job role names are a long way from being standardised. Pure writers of code for software systems are generally called *programmers* or *developers* or *engineers*. Sometimes these are prefixed by *junior, senior* or *principal* as status markers. But people endowed with the skill of programming can find themselves in many places within an organisation.

Most software development is related to *enterprise* software development. However, there are also many developer roles available in games development, mobile applications (apps), and embedded software development (software for microcontrollers in domestic appliances).

By kind permission of commitstrip.com

Lead Programmer

Software teams of more than a couple of people require someone to lead the team. The software team leader will generally (especially in agile software development) also be involved in the programming. They will have responsibility for managing the team – that is, making sure that they have the resources they need, and that they are happy and motivated. Clearly this is a role that not everyone is suited to, and this can provide a sticking point for career progression for programmers who just like programming and don't want to get involved in the *dark side*, as management is sometimes called.

Project Manager

Often working closely with a lead programmer, a project manager will be responsible for keeping the project on track. This role is often best done by someone with development experience, so that they understand the difficulties faced by the developers.

Architect

A technical architect is mostly concerned with defining the overall software structure and development processes of the system. They usually also end up managing the development team, at least in a technical sense. The solutions architect, will generally have a wider brief – evaluating and choosing the software technologies to use.

Designer

The word *designer* is often used ambiguously. The design of a system from the user's perspective is more properly called *requirements capture*. Designing how the screens should appear, and the system is navigated under various use cases, is often described as *design*.

The other use of the word *designer* is more to do with the designing the structure of the code. That is, what the database will look like, how the business logic will be represented in different classes and modules.

For external consumer-facing software products, the design will be very important, and may refer to a job much more concerned with the aesthetics of the product and the user experience (UX).

Support Agent

Software doesn't always work right, and the handling of support calls from internal or external customers can be a lot more than *have you tried turning it on and off again*. Although not a high-status software job, this is one of those roles from which able people may migrate, perhaps through software testing, into the development team. Indeed, the support team can provide valuable insights into bugs in the software as well as usability problems that need addressing, and will generally inform the whole software quality process.

Software Tester / Quality Control

Software testing may involve trying to reproduce possible bugs found by the support team, or it may involve proactively designing suites of automated tests to ensure that the code is as bug-free as possible before it is released.

Software testers generally have the skill of programming, and will have to write scripts and use automated testing software to look for bugs, or investigate bug reports before coordinating with the developers to fix problems. Software testing requires an eye for detail and a thorough and logical approach to problem solving.

By kind permission of commitstrip.com

The term *Quality Control* is perhaps a better way to think of this area of software development. Strategically, good quality control has a huge impact on an organisation's reputation, and should be a fundamental part of any development process.

Dev Ops

Perhaps the coolest sounding role is dev ops (Development and Operations). People who work in dev ops are more concerned with how software is deployed and kept working reliably in a live environment than in writing software systems themselves. Dev ops also need an appreciation of programming, as well as the ability to occasionally write scripts (small programs to automate some task) and familiarity with complex software deployment tools, as well as a good dose of responsibility. After all, no one wants problems with a live system.

Security Engineer

The internet is quite a hostile place, where criminals use programs that search for vulnerable web servers to hijack and hold hostage or hack to obtain information to sell. Keeping a computer network secure is a skill that organisations can't ignore.

Security is hard and requires a good knowledge of the technologies that are used to secure our networks.

Types of Organisation

Every organisation has its own take on software development and its own culture. When considering potential places to work, it's good to have some idea what to expect.

There are, of course, large differences in working culture between different countries as well. Figure 11.3 illustrates some of the differences between organisations, that might influence where you want to work.

Startups

Working for a startup can be enormously rewarding, but is also inherently risky. You may also find that a startup does not have things like a HR (Human Resource) department – or indeed any HR person. Working directly for a founder often means that the founder will expect you to have the same work ethic and ambition for the company that they have.

A start-up can rarely afford anything less than very high productivity and frequently, even though you may not know it, they might not know whether they can afford to pay you at the end of the month.

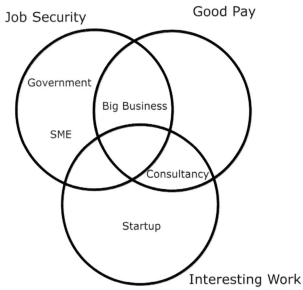

Figure 11.3. Job Security vs. Good Pay vs. Interesting Work.

On the other hand, being in at the ground floor of a successful startup can lead to rapid promotion and valuable stock-option opportunities, as well as having a much greater level of autonomy. An organised person might also find that they are the ones who get to develop the processes and procedures used by the company as it grows.

SMEs (Small and Medium Enterprises)

SMEs are generally taken to be between 50 and 250 employees and make up the majority of businesses in developed countries and many developing countries too.

Generally, unless the SME has a software product, its main focus is likely to be manufacturing something, or providing a specific service. From the management's perspective, the software is there to support the *core business*, and may not be as well funded or supported as a larger business – and wages will not usually be high.

However, as with startups, there are often more opportunities for career progression and the gaining of valuable experience and skills.

Consultancies

When large governmental or financial services organisations have a big project to do, they often supplement their in-house development teams with consultants. These consultants often come from large Consultancy or System Integrator companies that employ software people and then place them in organisations.

These consultancy companies charge a lot of money for their (or rather your) services. Working for one can be very rewarding, both financially and in training. In a consultancy you may find yourself working on a wide and varied range of projects.

The downside, is that you will often have to go where the work is, which is fine if you enjoy travel and meeting new people.

Big Businesses

Large companies of all sorts have their own in-house software teams that both support their own internal (for employees) and external (for customers') software systems. They also develop new projects, and will generally have a fairly well-established software development process and teams.

Although the work may have a tendency for dullness, there is usually considerable security here.

Flexible Working

The global COVID pandemic had a radical effect on working from home, or the coffee shop, or the park. For a while, working from home was pretty much the only option if organisations wanted to keep their software development going, and many software people got very used to working from home. These days, many organisations have tried to encourage their staff back into the office. However, a lasting legacy for many organisations is more openness to people working from home at least part of the time.

If this is something that is important to you, then you should definitely find out what your potential employer's attitude is to this. Many developers find that, because they are no longer having to suf-

By kind permission of commitstrip.com

fer a long commute, they will gladly share the extra time this creates, working longer hours when at home.

Software jobs are not really about attendance at work and, aside from the odd occasion where you really need to be around the same white-board, remote software development can work extremely well. Generally a happy employee is a productive employee.

Summary

In this final chapter, we have explored various routes into the software industry and what to expect when you get there.

If you have enjoyed this dive into the world of coding, then please continue your journey – whether it is finding that first job in software, or just enjoying the act of programming.

Glossary

API – Application Programming Interface. A software interface that allows one program to interact with another. For example, the system providing the API might be a web server and a web front end might call the API, using JSON as a file format.

Back-end – The server side of a system including the database and web server.

Bootstrap – A Javascript and CSS framework to make web pages look nice.

CLI – Command Line Interface. An interface to a system, based on typing in commands. The commands are often to generate code as a starting point for a project.

CSS – Cascading Style Sheets. A web technology that allows you to control the appearance of the elements of a web page.

DBA – DataBase Administrator. Someone who is responsible for the management and administration of a database, and often also involved in the design of database systems.

Front-end – Often used in the context of a type of developer. The user-interface layer of a system. Often it's web pages.

Full-stack – Often used In the context of a type of developer. The whole system from database to user interface.

git - Popular source code management software

HTML – HyperText Markup Language. The markup language used to render web pages.

int – short for integer (a whole number).

Iteration - repeating some code a number of times. In Python, using a `for` or `while` command.

Java - A programming language often used in large enterprise systems. Confusingly this language is very different from JavaScript.

JavaScript – A programming language included in most browsers that allows a web page to do clever stuff, like communicating with a web server, or special graphical effects.

JSON – JavaScript Object Notation. A text-based notation for transmitting structured data.

Linux - An open source computer operating system, like Microsoft Windows or Apple MacOS, but maintained as a community project and free of any license costs.

Migration – A small program that makes a change to a database, in a way that can be re-run whenever needed.

CRUD – Create Remove Update Delete. The things you generally need to do to data.

ORM – Object Relational Mapping. A framework that bridges the gap between a relational database and an object-oriented software system.

Relational Database - A database system based on tables of data.

Repo (repository) - A place for storing and managing source code files.

Pip – Pip installs packages. A tool for installing Python modules and programs.

Schema – The structure of a database, the definitions of the tables which it consists of.

Scope – The visibility of a variable. Where it can be accessed from.

SQL - Structured Query Language. A language for querying and modifying relational database.

SQLite - A small relational database system, ideal for learning about and experimenting with relational databases.

Static Pages - Pages served by a web server that are just files of HTML and do not have content that is generated dynamically.

State – Things that are recorded in a program generally in a variable.

TDD – Test Driven Development. A software engineering practice of writing unit tests before then writing code to make the test pass.

Unit Test - An automated test that tests one particular feature of some code.

Variable – a named piece of state.

Vue – A JavaScript framework for creating web front-ends.

Web Server - software that generates HTML web pages and *serves* them to a remote web browser.

Exercise Solutions

Exercise 2-1.

Write a program that asks the user to enter two numbers, and then display a message saying the numbers are the same only if they are the same.

```
a_str = input('Enter number a:')
a = int(a_str)

b_str = input('Enter number b:')
b = int(b_str)

if a == b:
    print('a and b are the same')
```

The numbers entered are changed into integers before comparing them using `int`, but they could be compared as string without being converted.

Exercise 2-2.

Write a program that asks the user to enter a password and then compares what they entered with a `saved_password` variable containing the string 'guessme' and print the message 'Password correct' or 'Password FAIL' depending on whether what was typed in matches or not.

```
saved_password = 'guessme'
```

183

```
password = input('Enter password:')

if saved_password == password:
    print('Password correct')
else:
    print('Password FAIL')
```

Exercise 2-3

The problem is to write a program that prompts the user to think of a number between 1 and 99 and the program then tries to guess the number by asking if the number is greater than a certain amount. Hint: *Lookup binary chop.*

```
print('Think of a number between 1 and 99')
low = 0
high = 100

while True:
    middle = round((high - low) / 2) + low
    print('{} {} {}'.format(low, middle, high))
    if middle == high or middle == low:
        break
    answer = input('Is the number greater than ' + str(middle))
    if (answer == 'y'):
        low = middle
    else:
        high = middle

print('Your number is ' + str(high))
```

The range of possible numbers is tracked using the `low` and `high` variables. A `middle` number is taken half way between `low` and `high`. If the number is greater than the `middle`, then `low` is set to be `middle` and a new `middle` chosen.

Exercise 3-1.

Write a short program that starts with an empty list and uses a `while` loop and the `input` command to keep prompting the user to enter a new movie title. Each time a new title is added, the list of titles should be printed. For a bonus, the program should exit if the title added is blank (its length is 0). Hint: the `break` command jumps out of a loop.

```
titles = []

while True:
    new_title = input('Enter a file title: ')
    if len(new_title) == 0:
```

```
        break
    titles.append(new_title)
    print(titles)
```

Exercise 3-2.

Starting with the code in *03_04_list_dict.py*, modify the program so that the movie's duration is printed after the movie title in parentheses.

```
movies = [
    {
        'title':'Jaws',
        'director':'Steven Spielberg',
        'duration': 124
    },
    {
        'title':'The Godfather',
        'director':'Francis Ford Coppola,',
        'duration': 175
    },
    {
        'title':'Baby Driver',
        'director':'Edgar Wright',
        'duration': 115
    },
]

for movie in movies:
    print(movie['title'] + ' (' + str(movie['duration']) + ' mins)')
```

Exercise 3-3.

Write a pointless program that puts all the numbers between 1 and 10,000,000 into a list. How long does it take for the program to run on your computer?

```
numbers = []

print("starting")
for x in range(1, 10000000):
    numbers.append(x)
print("finished")
```

You should find that it only takes a few seconds for your computer to count up to 10 million!

Exercise 4-1

Improve the appearance of the tic-tac-toe board by drawing bar between each position on the board and a line of underscores between

B. Exercise Solutions

each row.

```
board = ['.', '.', '.',
         '.', '.', '.',
         '.', '.', '.']

turn = 'x'

winning_lines = [[0, 1, 2], [3, 4, 5], [6, 7, 8], # horizontal
        [0, 3, 6], [1, 4, 7], [2, 5, 8], # vertical
        [0, 4, 8], [2, 4, 6]]            # diagonal

def show_board():
    print(board[0] + '|' + board[1] + '|' + board[2] + ' 1|2|3')
    print('---- ----')
    print(board[3] + '|' + board[4] + '|' + board[5] + ' 4|5|6')
    print('---- ----')
    print(board[6] + '|' + board[7] + '|' + board[8] + ' 7|8|9')

def check_winner():
    winner = '.' # no one
    for line in winning_lines:
        if board[line[0]] == board[line[1]] == board[line[2]]:
            winner = board[line[0]]
            break
    return winner

def allowed_moves():
    moves = []
    for move in range(1, 10):
        if board[move-1] == '.':
            moves.append(move)
    return moves

def get_move():
    position = -1 # un-chosen / no move available
    moves = allowed_moves()
    if len(moves) > 0:
        while position == -1:
            print()
            p_str = input('Move for ' + turn + str(moves) + ' :')
            p = int(p_str)
            if p in moves:
                position = p
    return position

show_board()

while True:
    position = get_move()
    if position == -1:
        print("Its a tie")
        break
    else:
        board[position-1] = turn
    show_board()
    winner = check_winner()
    if winner != '.':
        print(winner + ' wins!')
        break
    if turn == 'x':
        turn = 'o'
    else:
        turn = 'x'
```

Exercise 4-2

Change tic-tac-toe so that you play against the machine. The human player x starts first, and the machine playing o picks a free square at random.

```
import random

board = ['.', '.', '.',
         '.', '.', '.',
         '.', '.', '.']

turn = 'x'

winning_lines = [[0, 1, 2], [3, 4, 5], [6, 7, 8], # horizontal
        [0, 3, 6], [1, 4, 7], [2, 5, 8], # vertical
        [0, 4, 8], [2, 4, 6]]        # diagonal

def show_board():
    print(board[0] + '|' + board[1] + '|' + board[2] + ' 1|2|3')
    print('---- ----')
    print(board[3] + '|' + board[4] + '|' + board[5] + ' 4|5|6')
    print('---- ----')
    print(board[6] + '|' + board[7] + '|' + board[8] + ' 7|8|9')

def check_winner():
    winner = '.' # no one
    for line in winning_lines:
        if board[line[0]] == board[line[1]] == board[line[2]]:
            winner = board[line[0]]
            break
    return winner

def allowed_moves():
    moves = []
    for move in range(1, 10):
        if board[move-1] == '.':
            moves.append(move)
    return moves

def get_move():
    move = -1
    if turn == 'x':
        move = get_move_person()
    else:
        move = get_move_automatic()
        print(turn + ' move: ' + str(move))
    return move

def get_move_person():
    position = -1 # un-chosen / no move available
    moves = allowed_moves()
    if len(moves) > 0:
        while position == -1:
            print()
            p_str = input('Move for ' + turn + str(moves) + ' :')
            p = int(p_str)
            if p in moves:
                position = p
    return position

def get_move_automatic():
    moves = allowed_moves()
    move = random.choice(moves)
    return move

show_board()

while True:
    position = get_move()
    if position == -1:
        print("Its a tie")
```

```
            break
        else:
            board[position-1] = turn
        show_board()
        winner = check_winner()
        if  winner != '.':
            print(winner + ' wins!')
            break
        if turn == 'x':
            turn = 'o'
        else:
            turn = 'x'
```

New functions `get_move_person` and `get_move_automatic` are defined. Because we have the function `allowed_moves`, we can just pick one of the moves in the list.

Exercise 4-3

Improve the automatic play so that if a winning move it is taken, or if there is a move that blocks x from winning then take that move, otherwise pick a move at random.

```
import random

board = ['.', '.', '.',
         '.', '.', '.',
         '.', '.', '.']

turn = 'x'

winning_lines = [[0, 1, 2], [3, 4, 5], [6, 7, 8], # horizontal
                 [0, 3, 6], [1, 4, 7], [2, 5, 8], # vertical
                 [0, 4, 8], [2, 4, 6]]            # diagonal

def show_board():
    print()
    print(board[0] + '|' + board[1] + '|' + board[2] + '  1|2|3')
    print('---- ----')
    print(board[3] + '|' + board[4] + '|' + board[5] + '  4|5|6')
    print('---- ----')
    print(board[6] + '|' + board[7] + '|' + board[8] + '  7|8|9')
    print()

def check_winner():
    winner = '.' # no one
    for line in winning_lines:
        if board[line[0]] == board[line[1]] == board[line[2]]:
            winner = board[line[0]]
            break
    return winner

def allowed_moves():
    moves = []
    for move in range(1, 10):
        if board[move-1] == '.':
            moves.append(move)
    return moves

def get_move():
    move = -1
    if turn == 'x':
        move = get_move_person()
    else:
        move = get_move_automatic()
```

188

```python
        if move != -1:
            print(turn + ' moves: ' + str(move))
    return move

def get_move_person():
    position = -1 # un-chosen / no move available
    moves = allowed_moves()
    if len(moves) > 0:
        while position == -1:
            print()
            p_str = input('Move for ' + turn + str(moves) + ' :')
            p = int(p_str)
            if p in moves:
                position = p
    return position

def is_winning_move(board_position, turn):
    result = False
    old_contents = board[board_position-1]
    board[board_position-1] = turn
    for line in winning_lines:
        if board[line[0]] == board[line[1]] == board[line[2]]:
            if board[line[0]] == turn:
                result = True
                break
    board[board_position-1] = old_contents # put it back
    return result

def get_move_automatic():
    moves = allowed_moves()
    if len(moves) == 0:
        return -1
    # look for winning move
    for move in moves:
        if is_winning_move(move, 'o'):
            return move
    # look for blocking move
    for move in moves:
        if is_winning_move(move, 'x'):
            return move
    return random.choice(moves)

show_board()

while True:
    position = get_move()
    if position == -1:
        print("Its a tie")
        break
    else:
        board[position-1] = turn
    show_board()
    winner = check_winner()
    if  winner != '.':
        print(winner + ' wins!')
        break
    if turn == 'x':
        turn = 'o'
    else:
        turn = 'x'
```

The new `get_move_automatic` makes use of the `is_winning_move` function first to see if the automatic player can win, and then to see if it can block a winning move from its opponent, and as a final option choses a move at random.

Exercise 4-4

If you feel slightly uneasy about the function `check_winner`, then that's because it has a bug in it. Take a moment to work through it carefully, thinking about what happens if it finds a row of '.' before it finds a row of 'x' or 'o' on the board. There is an improved version of the function and explanation in the example answer for this exercise.

```
board = ['.', '.', '.',
         '.', '.', '.',
         'x', 'x', 'x']

winning_lines = [[0, 1, 2], [3, 4, 5], [6, 7, 8], # horizontal
        [0, 3, 6], [1, 4, 7], [2, 5, 8], # vertical
        [0, 4, 8], [2, 4, 6]]          # diagonal


#buggy original check_winner function.
def check_winner1():
    winner = '.' # no one
    for line in winning_lines:
        if board[line[0]] == board[line[1]] == board[line[2]]:
            winner = board[line[0]]
            break
    return winner

#fixed - only check for rows of x or o
def check_winner2():
    winner = '.' # no one
    for line in winning_lines:
        if board[line[0]] != '.' and (board[line[0]] == board[line[1]] == board[line[2]]):
            winner = board[line[0]]
            break
    return winner

print(check_winner1())
print(check_winner2())
```

The flaw with `check_winner` is that if it finds a row of . before it finds a row of *x* or *o* then it will return . as a winner.

The fix is to add an extra clause in the `if` statements condition to make sure that the first line position isn't a .. That is, the line must be either *x* or *o*.

Exercise 5-1. Define a class to represent a Person

Define a class to represent a `person`, that has instance variables on `first_name` and `surname`. Define a method called `full_name` that returns both parts of the name.

```
class Person:

    def __init__(self, first_name, surname):
        self.first_name = first_name
        self.surname = surname
```

```
    def full_name(self):
        return self.first_name + ' ' + self.surname


p = Person('Simon', 'Monk')
print(p.full_name())
```

Exercise 5-2

Define a class to represent an Employee.

Create a subclasss of Person called Employee that is a subclass of
Person and adds a new variable salary and defines a method called
give_rise that takes a percentage and increases the salary when
called.

```
class Person:

    def __init__(self, first_name, surname):
        self.first_name = first_name
        self.surname = surname

    def full_name(self):
        return self.first_name + ' ' + self.surname

class Employee(Person):

    def __init__(self, first_name, surname, salary):
        Person.__init__(self, first_name, surname)
        self.salary = salary

    def give_rise(self, percent):
        self.salary += self.salary * percent / 100


p = Employee('Simon', 'Monk', 100)
p.give_rise(10)
print(p.salary)
```

Exercise 6-1.

Add some code to *blackjack_final.py* so that if the player sticks, then
the next 5 cards that would be drawn are displayed.

```
from card import *
from deck import *

def score_hand(cards):
    score = 0
    have_ace = False
    for card in cards:
        if card.is_ace():
            have_ace = True
        score += card.value()
        if score > 21 and have_ace:
            score -= 10 # lower ace value
            have_ace = False # only do this once
    return score
```

```
def display_hand(hand):
    score = score_hand(hand)
    print('Your hand: ' + str(hand) + ' (' + str(score) + ')')

def play_game():
    deck = Deck()
    deck.shuffle()
    hand = []
    deck.deal(2, hand)
    print('\n\nNew Game')

    while True:
        score = score_hand(hand)
        display_hand(hand)
        action = input('t-twist or s-stick: ')
        if action == 't':
            deck.deal(1, hand)
            score = score_hand(hand)
            if score > 21:
                display_hand(hand)
                print('BUST!')
                break
        elif action == 's':
            print('Sticking with :' + str(score))
            print('Next 5 cards: ' + str(deck.cards[:5]))
            break

while True:
    play_game()
```

The next 5 cards of the deck are found using `deck.cards[:5]`. You can also include the first index position by writing `deck.cards[0:5]`. Both will do the same thing.

Exercise 6-2.

Modify *blackjack_final.py* so that rather than start a new deck of cards for each hand, the same deck is used until all the cards have gone.

```
from card import *
from deck import *

def score_hand(cards):
    score = 0
    have_ace = False
    for card in cards:
        if card.is_ace():
            have_ace = True
        score += card.value()
        if score > 21 and have_ace:
            score -= 10 # lower ace value
            have_ace = False # only do this once
    return score

def display_hand(hand):
    score = score_hand(hand)
    print('Your hand: ' + str(hand) + ' (' + str(score) + ')')

def play_game():
    hand = []
    deck.deal(2, hand)
    print('\n\nNew Game')
    print(str(len(deck.cards)) + ' cards left')
```

```
    while True:
        score = score_hand(hand)
        display_hand(hand)
        action = input('t-twist or s-stick: ')
        if action == 't':
            if len(deck.cards) < 1:
                print('Run out of cards!')
                return
            deck.deal(1, hand)
            score = score_hand(hand)
            if score > 21:
                display_hand(hand)
                print('BUST!')
                break
        elif action == 's':
            print('Sticking with :' + str(score))
            break

deck = Deck()
deck.shuffle()

while len(deck.cards) >= 2:
    play_game()
```

The main change is that `deck = Deck()` and `deck.shuffle()` are moved outside the `play_game` function.

Also when you twist, a new if statement (`if len(deck.cards)< 1:`) makes sure that there is a card left in the deck to be dealt.

Exercise 6-3

Modify *blackjack_final.py* so that printing occurs in a ticker-type way, where there is a short delay between each letter of the text being printed. Hint: search for python print without new line and Python `time.sleep`.

```
from card import *
from deck import *
from time import sleep

def score_hand(cards):
    score = 0
    have_ace = False
    for card in cards:
        if card.is_ace():
            have_ace = True
        score += card.value()
        if score > 21 and have_ace:
            score -= 10 # lower ace value
            have_ace = False # only do this once
    return score

def print_slow(message):
    for character in message:
        print(character, end='')
        sleep(0.05)
    print()

def display_hand(hand):
    score = score_hand(hand)
    print_slow('Your hand: ' + str(hand) + ' (' + str(score) + ')')
```

```
def play_game():
    hand = []
    deck.deal(2, hand)
    print_slow('\n\nNew Game')
    print_slow(str(len(deck.cards)) + ' cards left')
    while True:
        score = score_hand(hand)
        display_hand(hand)
        action = input('t-twist or s-stick: ')
        if action == 't':
            if len(deck.cards) < 1:
                print_slow('Run out of cards!')
                return
            deck.deal(1, hand)
            score = score_hand(hand)
            if score > 21:
                display_hand(hand)
                print_slow('BUST!')
                break
        elif action == 's':
            print_slow('Sticking with :' + str(score))
            break

deck = Deck()
deck.shuffle()

while len(deck.cards) >= 2:
    play_game()
```

The function `print_slow` uses 'print(character, end=")' to print a character without a line feed.

Exercise 6-4

Modify the tic-tac-toe game from Chapter 4, (*04_10_xo_5.py*) so that it does not crash if someone enters a move position that is not a number.

```
board = [' ', ' ', ' ',
         ' ', ' ', ' ',
         ' ', ' ', ' ']

turn = 'x'

winning_lines = [[0, 1, 2], [3, 4, 5], [6, 7, 8], # horizontal
        [0, 3, 6], [1, 4, 7], [2, 5, 8], # vertical
        [0, 4, 8], [2, 4, 6]]        # diagonal

def show_board():
    print(board[0] + board[1] + board[2] + ' 123')
    print(board[3] + board[4] + board[5] + ' 456')
    print(board[6] + board[7] + board[8] + ' 789')

def check_winner():
    winner = ' ' # no one
    for line in winning_lines:
        if board[line[0]] == board[line[1]] == board[line[2]]:
            winner = board[line[0]]
            break
    return winner

def allowed_moves():
    moves = []
    for move in range(1, 10):
        if board[move-1] == ' ':
            moves.append(move)
```

```
    return moves

def get_move():
    position = -1 # un-chosen / no move available
    moves = allowed_moves()
    if len(moves) > 0:
        while position == -1:
            p_str = input('Move for ' + turn + str(moves) + ' :')
            try:
                p = int(p_str)
                if p in moves:
                    position = p
            except:
                pass
    return position

show_board()

while True:
    position = get_move()
    if position == -1:
        print("Its a tie")
        break
    else:
        board[position-1] = turn
    show_board()
    winner = check_winner()
    if winner != '.':
        print(winner + ' wins!')
        break
    if turn == 'x':
        turn = 'o'
    else:
        turn = 'x'
```

The `get_move` function now makes use of a `try/except` block to catch any error if a number is not entered.

Exercise 7-1.

Extend the following query, so that is also displays the name of the film's director.

```
select title, duration from movie_titles where duration > 120;
```

```
select movie_titles.title, directors.name, movie_titles.duration
from movie_titles, directors
where movie_titles.duration > 120
and directors.id = movie_titles.director_id;
```

To do this, we join the `movie_titles` and `directors` tables.

Exercise 7-2.

Write a Python program using the sqlite3 module to print each director and the number of films credited to them in the test database.

```
\section*{ run from same directory as test_db.sqlite3}

import sqlite3
connection = sqlite3.connect('test_db.sqlite3')
cursor = connection.cursor()

for row in cursor.execute('SELECT id, name FROM directors'):
    id, name = row
    movies_cursor = connection.cursor()
    movies_cursor.execute('SELECT COUNT(*) FROM movie_titles WHERE director_id = ' + str(id))
    movies_count = movies_cursor.fetchone()[0]
    print(name + " " + str(movies_count))
```

Exercise 10-1

Add another test for the `deal` method, that checks that when one card is dealt the card is no longer in the deck.

Hint, PyUnit has a `assertNotIn` method.

```
import unittest
from deck import Deck

class TestDeck(unittest.TestCase):

    def test_deal(self):
        d = Deck()
        hand = []
        d.deal(1, hand)
        self.assertEqual(len(d.cards), 51, "incorrect deck size after dealing")
        self.assertEqual(len(hand), 1, "incorrect hand size after dealing")
        self.assertNotIn(hand[0], d.cards, "dealt card still in deck")

unittest.main()
```

The `assertNotIn` method takes a list as its first parameter and something to search for in the list as its second parameter. The third parameter being the message to be displayed if the assertion fails.

You can find documentation on the various types of *assert* in the PyUnit documentation here: https://docs.python.org/3/library/unittest.html

Exercise 10-2

Write a test for the `shuffle` method.

Hint: This is difficult, because of the random nature of the shuffle method. But a reasonable test might be to have two decks, one shuffled and one not. Then compare the cards before and after shuffling and make sure that no more than 5 of them are at the same place in the deck. You may find `assertLess` useful.

```python
import unittest
from deck import Deck

class TestDeck(unittest.TestCase):

    def test_deal(self):
        d1 = Deck()
        d1.shuffle()
        d2 = Deck()
        num_matches = 0
        for i in range(0, 52):
            if d1.cards[i] == d2.cards[i]:
                num_matches += 1
        self.assertLess(num_matches, 5, "deck doesn't look shuffled well matches: " +
            str(num_matches))

unittest.main()
```

The test creates two decks (`d1` and `d2`) and shuffles just `d1`. It then goes though each card position, adding 1 to `num_matches` if the cards are the same. This is not an ideal test, as it could very occasionally fail just by chance. For 5 cards to be the same, the probability would be 1 in: $52^5 = 380{,}204{,}032$ .. which are odds we can live with, as we are getting into territory where the test is more likely to fail because of the computer being struck by lightening than a fluke deal.

https://math.stackexchange.com/questions/204407

Index

Biography

Simon Monk has written over twenty titles on programming and electronics and has sold over 750,000 books that have been translated into ten different languages. You can find out more about his books here: `http://simonmonk.org`.

Simon has a bachelor's degree in Computer Science and Cybernetics and a doctorate in Software Engineering. He has worked in many industries as a software developer and also pursues his interest in hobby electronics through the company MonkMakes Ltd (`https://monkmakes.com`).

He lives in the North West of England. You can follow him on Twitter, where he is @simonmonk2

Printed in Great Britain
by Amazon

38645356R00119